GW00648098

Copyright © M Publishing 2014

All rights reserved

No part of this publication may be reproduced, stored in or introduced into a
retrieval system, or transmitted, in any form, or by any means (electronic, mechanical,
photocopying, recording, or otherwise) without the prior written permission of the
copyright owner.

Artwork:
Zorica and Dragan Jovanovic Ignjatov (zodrag@gmail.com)
Jana Sooz (http://soozlillend.deviantart.com)

Copyediting:
Barbara Murray

Published by
M PUBLISHING

Second Edition 2015

Printed by
Lightning Source, UK

A catalogue record for this book is available from the British Library

ISBN
978-1-909323-77-3

THE SEED

on a 7x7 evolutionary trajectory

By

milena

M PUBLISHING

CONTENTS

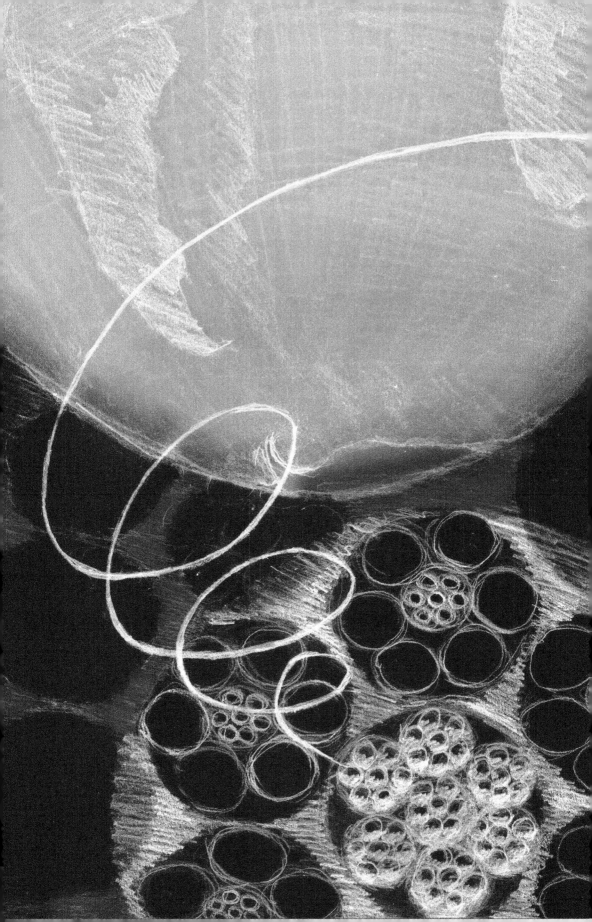

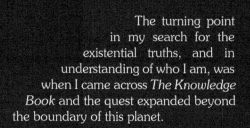

The turning point in my search for the existential truths, and in understanding of who I am, was when I came across *The Knowledge Book* and the quest expanded beyond the boundary of this planet.

If I myself am a book, until I learn letters I will not be able to read it and so to learn about myself. Now I am aware that the missing letters are from the cosmic alphabet of truth. They are vibrational keys able to unlock the secrets of the universe, of life and of my own self.

In this book, which you hold in your hands, you will find the thought lines fortified by the energy/information from *The Knowledge Book* – since from reading and studying *The Knowledge Book* some of its frequencies have become an organic part of my being. However, these frequencies are not mine. They belong to humanity and I am grateful for this opportunity to share them with you – though from my personal coordinates.

Since the fresh cosmic energy that comes to our planet continuously converts into new information and knowledge, everything written in this book is inevitably subject to upgrading. Despite this transient nature of knowledge, I hope you find reading this book a valuable experience,

Milena

WHY DYING,
WHY REINCARNATING

Are we just terrestrial?

Are we solely a result of the unification of our mother's and father's genes? Or is there yet another element involved; should we consider the model of the Trinity as fundamental to the formation processes?

In the monotheistic religions, the Triune God is a symbol of Three co-equal Essences being One. If we mirror this Three-are-One pattern, we could wonder where the third gene, to complete a foetus, comes from – from the Earth or from the sky?

Chain of incarnations

Whether a human being is granted one life, or a chain of lives, is still a subject of dispute amongst individuals and social groups on Earth.

If reincarnation is a programme whereupon energy is epitomised as different bodies at different times, what would be the meaning of accumulating those experiences? Perhaps, as a result of numerous life opportunities, a human being is meant to evolve into a perfect, omnipotent body, incombustible and able to last forever – simply due to their genetic potential? This, taken as a truth, would indicate that the dying of an entity, associated with the programme of reincarnation, is just a temporary phenomenon. Each living and each dying would consequently serve as steps towards the immortal body, inhabited by an evolving energy.

Following this premise, if we are an energy that currently experiences its own evolution within a crude-matter form called HUMAN, there must be a point on our journey when we acquire properties of an immortal being.

Present
reality is that the
physical cells of our
body lose their potential
during our life on Earth, and
our body eventually becomes
unusable. The terrestrial body
thus ends up being buried
or burnt, and our tangible
physical aspects merge
with the planetary
biosphere.

At the
event of death,
the energy potential that
worked through our body
ascends towards celestial stations,
where it has come from as a direct
off-planetary element of the foetus.
In the celestial laboratories then, it
waits for the most suitable time to
continue to evolve through another
body. We can therefore say that a
particular aspect of ourselves
survives our personal
death.

If
immortality is
our true evolutionary
target, an immortal human
must be of a specific biological
constitution, with a bigger brain
power and higher consciousness.
Hence, for as long as we go
from incarnation to
incarnation, we continue
working on acquiring
those qualities.

In that process, each of our cells receives
its essence-energy aiming to reach saturation with
it. Equally so, our cellular consciousness develops to
the consciousness level of our brain, and each bodily
cell transforms into a cell-brain. Upon this completion,
we are no longer subject to dying, but to immortality.
In order to carry on life's duties relevant to such a
level of evolvement, we will travel interplanetary
distances by our mature body of light.

Immortality

Would it make sense that the Power,
which produced the programme of
existence, established the rules and provided
the mechanisms for a continuous monitoring of all
aspects of the creation, with the objective to run that
programme most successfully? If so, then life on Earth
has started and is perpetuated through an application of the
existential ordinances, whether here we are aware of them or not.

In accordance with these ordinances, cosmic influences fortify our
planet in the direction congruent with its cosmic destiny. Thus our
planetary energy medium, fed and supervised by the technological
powers of the higher realities, triggers necessary evolutionary processes
in all life-forms on Earth.

In this way, our gradual preparation for immortality, and the dimensions
beyond that evolutionary stage, has been taking place on Earth and is
equally available to everyone. However, this very fact does not make it easier
to understand the variety of evolutionary levels exhibited by humans, and the
certainty that we are still dying.

One can therefore ask whether we are really meant to stop dying. Or, if we can
turn into immortal beings, how far that threshold is from us? By pondering those
questions, information will be revealed in a scope each one of us is ready for.

My sincere wish is that this book inspires you in your search for truth.

Milena

INFINITE

CONSCIOUSNESS

dying →

reincarnating →

11

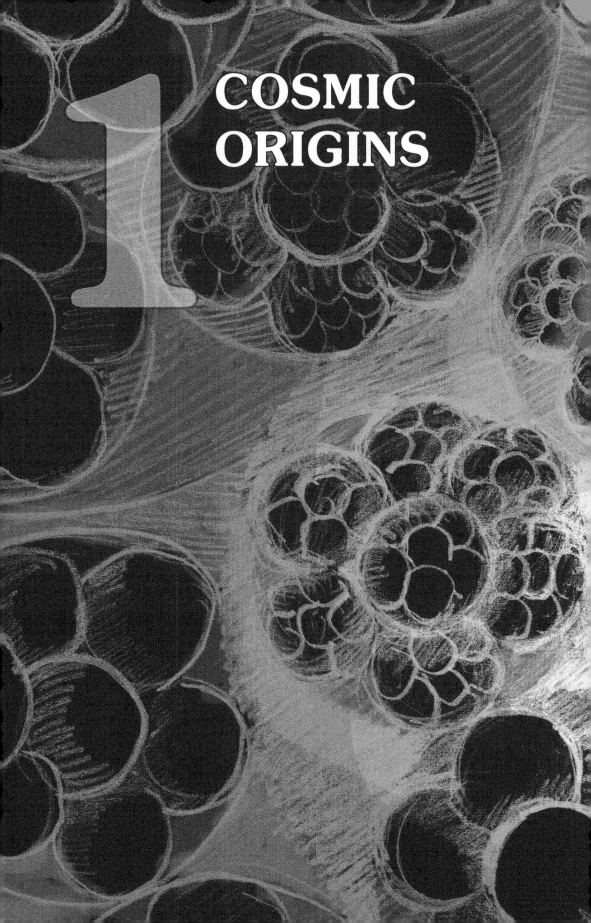

1 COSMIC ORIGINS

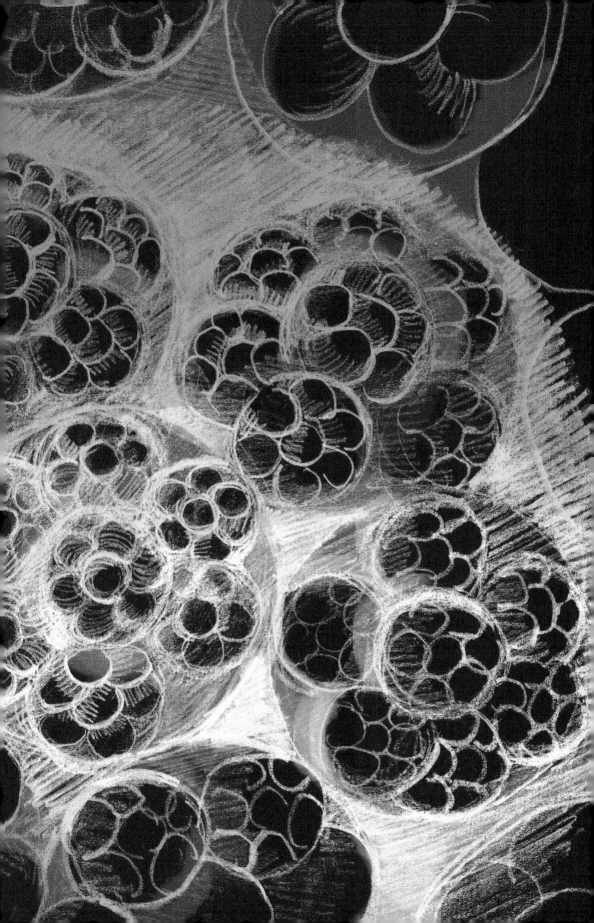

THE SEED IS A BIOLOGICAL COMPUTER

Life starts from a seed. A seed is a natural energy, programmed to unfold its treasures by processing the influences of a given medium. It is a biological universal computer, loaded with the intelligence and the might of the Creator.

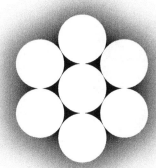

Take a seed of a plant! It requires a source of nutrients (light, soil, water) to sprout and grow, till the completion of its cycle. A new seed is then produced, to perpetuate the programme of the given species.

A human being develops from a seed engrafted with the essence-energy of the Creator. That essence-energy is fundamental to the developing of all our powers. We are destined to crave it and ultimately to fill each of our cells with it.

At the peak of our evolution, we manifest the properties of essence-energy within our material body. Consequently, we become the possessors of an everlasting, immortal, body. Having claimed sufficient essence-energy from the universal depths, which belongs to it, only then does our body become REAL.

Life on our planet is a training and testing medium that prepares us for *our real dimension*[1]. We are led to that dimension through the evolution of our *essence-gene*[2].

Through the programme of the essence-gene, human material form is fertilised with spiritual values till it reaches its predestined perfection.

SEEDS FROM THE SAME ESSENCE

Humans have come into existence from the essence-energy of the Creator. Thus all of us are seeds that share the same *essence*[3], and have equal potential of godly proportions.

The speck of essence-energy, initially engrafted to a human seed, is of an off-planetary origin. It means that we live on this planet but, essentially, we are not from it. In other words – we are extra-terrestrials.

Here, at the cosmic school on Earth, classes on self-development do not stop. They are subject to *celestial influences*[4] and supervision. The aim is the activation of our full genetic potential, and so of our essence-power. From the beginning of the 20th century, special cosmic energy is directed towards Earth to speed up that process.

With strong enough brain power, we can receive those cosmic energies as well as claim essence-energy directly from the Spiritual totality. The *cosmic currents*[5] showering the planet reinforce our life-potential, and are instrumental in the evolution of our consciousness. Thus, gradually, owing primarily to the activity of our *brain*[6], our physical cells are being revitalised and prepared for *immortality*[7].

Each human evolves through a particular energy dimension, amongst myriad dimensions present in the orders of evolution. Hence from all the cosmic pores, which arrive on Earth and carry innumerable information, it is necessary that we reach those coming from the dimension whose evolution we go through.

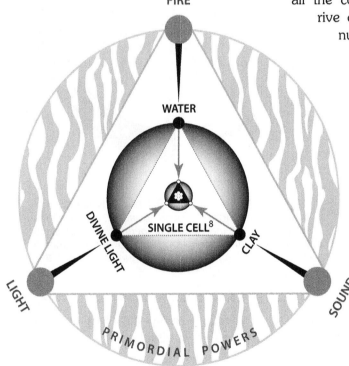

When our cellular energy, saturated with essence-energy, and our cerebral energy are at the same coordinates and join forces, we will be able to create everything we think of – even new planets and life-forms on them.

Such is the potential of a godly seed.

15

ALPHA AND BETA ENERGIES

To complete its evolution, a human seed needs to receive godly and spiritual energies and evolve through them.

Godly energy is alpha energy, energy of love; and is linked to the colour white. The entire life-medium on Earth is a medium of godly energy.

Spiritual energy is beta energy associated with logic, intellect and consciousness. It is the essence-energy that belongs to us by the virtue of our blueprint. Linked to the colour black, beta energy comes from the heights of the universal dimensions – from the *Spiritual totality*[9]. We are connected to that totality by an energy link called the *silver cord*, which is attached to our brain.

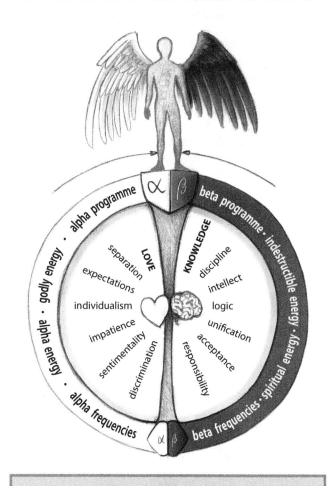

Everyone should consider his body as a priceless gift from one whom he loves above all, a marvelous work of art, of indescribable beauty, and mystery beyond human conception, and so delicate that a word, a breath, a look, nay, a thought may injure it.

– Nikola Tesla

In order to receive spiritual energy, we need to purify ourselves and make necessary evolvements. For this reason, we obtain spiritual energy according to our evolutionary level.

Climbing to the altitude of our full genetic potential depends on our capacity to attract and assimilate energies that are celestially specified for such an achievement. Both our bodily constitution and our personality follow this frequency ascension.

SPIRITUAL TOTALITY

SPIRIT[10] is a totality
of an everlasting natural energy.
This energy is our primal life-source.

Human essence-power dwells
in the Spiritual totality,
until we gradually claim it.

is a natural power.
The *Spiritual Plan*[11] reflects the
energy intensity of this totality by
appropriating it to each
evolutionary dimension and
so evolves individuals

3. In an event of *death*[12],
the silver cord
is disconnected
from our body.
At the same time, it elevates
our essence-gene up to the dimension,
the consciousness level of which
we have achieved.

Through this energy
cord we also make
astral journeys[13]

(spiritual) SILVER CORD[14]

7. From that level, marked as the
7th Evolutionary dimension,
a human being continues to progress
towards an infinite awareness and an
infinite consciousness

6. Such humans are considered
perfect human beings. As a microcosm,
each one of them summarises the
macrocosm in their physical vessel and
lives in unity with the macrocosm.

5. When we fully complement our physical
body with the essence-energy from
the Spiritual totality, our physical body
merges with its abstract body and
becomes REAL and immortal

4. We can claim spiritual energy,
(essence-energy),
according to the Spiritual Plan,
only if we can receive
the energy from the
12th Evolutionary dimension[15]

2. We need numerous
INCARNATIONS
in order to draw the
spiritual energy,
from the Spiritual totality,
that belongs to us

1. By the silver cord, attached to our brain,
each human being is connected to a
section of the Spiritual totality and
evolves through the frequency range
of their particular dimension

It is through the growing power of our thoughts that we claim our
genuine being from the Spiritual totality

When a human seed fully receives its essence-energy, it reaches its own essence-qualities and blossoms into essence-consciousness. It finds itself and simultaneously loses its individuality, by becoming one with the Whole. As the possessors of their essence-power, those humans observe everything from the coordinates of the essence – rather than through their eyes. With the love from the essence, they embrace the entire creation and happily contribute to its prosperity.

EVOLVEMENT GENERATES RESPONSIBILITY

The application of universal laws and evolutionary ordinances onto existential dimensions, benefits the evolvement of all seeds and empowers them to actualise their genetic potential.

The continuous reflections from higher dimensions are lights and divine lights sent along evolutionary scales. A seed, able to receive and utilise them, goes through its own transformation and gradually progresses on the evolutionary path. Such a seed will eventually complete the evolution of its essence and then, from the coordinates of the essence, start to reflect evolutionary energy onto its own surrounding. Each of our *64 billion cells*[16] works hard towards this completion.

A human seed, which has achieved the level of its genetic fulfilment, called a *perfect human*[17], consequently undertakes a conscious responsibility within the orders of the universe. That transition happens organically, after an individual becomes fully cognisant of the sovereignty of the universal laws that ceaselessly propagate an order, harmony and unity. To follow these universal laws – out of mere respect and gratitude for that very opportunity – thence becomes an existential purpose, as well as a universal duty. This is the level of universal truth, grasped and lived by a particle that has become an entity and traversed the distance from micro- to macro-consciousness.

ENVIRONMENTAL INFLUENCES

According to the evolutionary ordinances, in the realm of time and space, every seed dwells in the medium of energies most suitable to its evolutionary level.

> *The Human is no exception to the natural order. Man, like the Universe, is a machine. Nothing enters our minds or determines our actions which is not directly or indirectly a response to stimuli beating upon our sense organs from without. – Nikola Tesla*

As well as responding to the influences from the immediate environment, a seed is also meant to respond to the celestial lights (compulsory evolutionary energy/information from the cosmic curriculum). If the seed cannot withstand the celestial lights and benefit from them, it is in danger of prematurely terminating its life on the given evolutionary level.

The extent to which a seed will benefit from celestial influences depends on the perception and the consciousness level of each seed. Even though the evolutionary triggers are from outside, the capacity and effort to evolve come from inside a seed and reflect the ability of the seed to follow its genetic programme. If a seed does not change, adapt and therefore evolve, being assisted by these external influences, the seed will not blossom and produce its fruits.

The influence that an environment makes on any seed is indisputable. The responses to those influences hugely affect what qualities, amongst the genetic potential of a seed, are going to be manifested.

Modern molecular biology and genetics have discovered that the genetic material of an organism (genome) is flexible, and that resolutions to outside influences are built into the genome and even passed to next generation as acquired property. This behaviour of a genome, which negotiates with the environment and consequently naturally self-modifies, is a perfect model of a circular causation.

Science has explained the influences of terrestrial environment on our biology, and on the shaping our personality, at length. Even identical twins will develop differently, if separated and placed in different families. The way they evolve, in the given mediums, will be memorised by their genetic material and that environmentally triggered change of the genome will be relayed to the following generation.

ORIGIN OF THE SEED

Seed carries a cosmic programme

Let us ask ourselves some questions! Who has placed the seed of life and nature, or the human seed, on Earth and elsewhere? What is the Power that enabled the formation of matter and universes, and gives thought and feelings to matter? Can that Power ever detach Itself from Its own creation? Furthermore, how is life on Earth affected by the wider cosmic environment of more complex celestial structures such as *the solar system[18], the galaxy, a galaxy-cluster, a universe-cluster[19]*, and so on, in which Earth as the natural flying saucer is embedded? The thought capacity of humans and the technology on this planet will need to evolve significantly more, to enable explicit scientific answers to those questions.

However, what is obvious is that nature provides the necessary setting for life on Earth and so for the presence of human beings on it. But what is nature? Is it not a specific programme written by the Creator, and supervised through the system of His *celestial hierarchy[20]*?

The human seed, which also springs out of the Creator's designs, is prepared and programmed in the cosmic laboratories. From there, as a soul-seed, it is sent to the *Dimension of Evolution[21]* where, starting as a foetus, the soul-seed takes its life course in conjunction with the ordinances of evolution. What we call destiny is an unfolding of an individual's life programme.

SOUL-SEED[22] is the result of a triple action:
(1) – the LORDLY ORDER creates a biological cell;
(2) – the PRE-EMINENT MOTHER (SPIRITUAL PLAN) connects it to the spiritual energy while
(3) – the CREATOR completes the seed by infusing it with HIS essence-energy.
In its constitution, the seed reflects the orders of the higher realities.

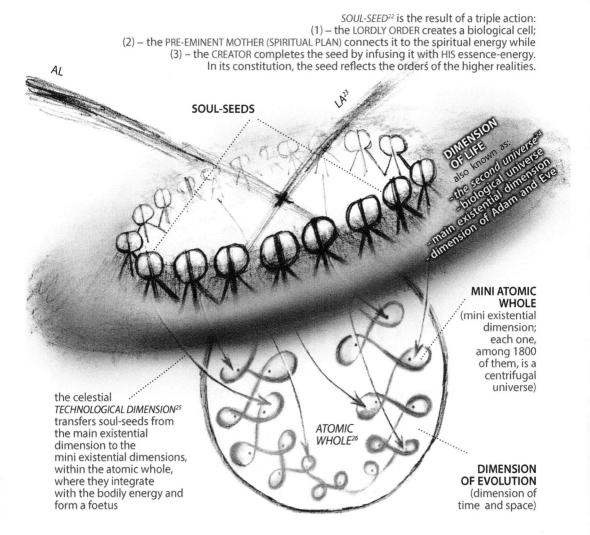

AL

SOUL-SEEDS

LA[23]

DIMENSION OF LIFE
also known as:
- the second universe[24]
- biological universe
- main existential dimension
- dimension of Adam and Eve

MINI ATOMIC WHOLE
(mini existential dimension; each one, among 1800 of them, is a centrifugal universe)

the celestial TECHNOLOGICAL DIMENSION[25] transfers soul-seeds from the main existential dimension to the mini existential dimensions, within the atomic whole, where they integrate with the bodily energy and form a foetus

ATOMIC WHOLE[26]

DIMENSION OF EVOLUTION
(dimension of time and space)

The human seed has spiritual, physical and thought energy properties inherent in it. We therefore simultaneously progress through these three fields.

Our spiritual evolvement takes place through spiritual energy, which is a *natural energy*[29] (essence-energy). Even our physical vehicle gets more perfect as our capacity to receive spiritual energy grows. Hence by holding more spiritual energy within our cells, we become more powerful – both spiritually and physically.

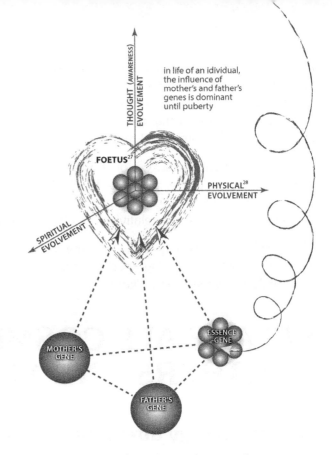

in life of an idividual, the influence of mother's and father's genes is dominant until puberty

THOUGHT (AWARENESS) EVOLVEMENT

FOETUS[27]

PHYSICAL[28] EVOLVEMENT

SPIRITUAL EVOLVEMENT

ESSENCE GENE

MOTHER'S GENE

FATHER'S GENE

We attract spiritual energy by thought. As our thought evolves, its frequency is elevated. As a consequence, our awareness expands. The broader the awareness, the bigger is the base for our consciousness.

> *Most persons are so absorbed in the contemplation of the outside world that they are wholly oblivious to what is passing on within themselves. The premature death of millions is primarily traceable to this cause. Even among those who exercise care, it is a common mistake to avoid imaginary, and ignore the real dangers. And confessed: The opinion of the world does not affect me. I have placed as the real values in my life, what follows when I am dead. – Nikola Tesla*

Rejecting the unknown

At the *evolutionary dimension*[30] experienced on our planet, visible crude matter is arranged in a seemingly endless number of settings to induce our necessary experiences. Hence, we easily get caught in an illusion that all that matters ends with the material world. However, our experiences gradually indicate a bigger picture of reality – one that stretches beyond what we can perceive.

If we deny other existential dimensions, we indirectly postulate that only the life-forms present on our planet are possible and real; as the entire realm of life modalities that are unknown to us does not exist. Denying something we do not know about, or for that reason classifying it as impossible and untrue, is an attitude of a rather provincial mind.

On the other hand, what we on Earth consider being real or a truth, might well not be so in universal terms. It might appear as such, only to our level of perception and awareness. If we therefore accept that our perception and awareness evolve, we can relativise our observations and conclusions.

There is always a next higher plane in the scales of infinite awareness, and each stage is earned by climbing specific energy steps. The chart of those energy scales belongs to the *Divine Plan*[31].

WE ARE ALL COSMIC BROTHERS AND SISTERS

Cosmic energy alters our genes

Human genes are magnificent cosmic formulae that carry the life programme of an entity. They unfold godly potential in the realms of crude matter.

Parallel to their evolutionary capacity in a given incarnation, genes read information of the medium they are sent into and determine the best response to the circumstances. In this mechanism, an unavoidable influential element is of celestial origin. It is the cosmic energy present on the planet.

Owing to the influences of those higher realities and the programme of nature, energy on Earth continuously changes. Nowadays the special cosmic energy, sent to our planet via celestial technology, has the power to make us evolve in an unprecedented way in one lifetime. This energy accelerates the alteration of our DNA and can even change our blood type.

Our genuine personality (a perfect human) is concealed within our essence, and the process of reaching it is programmed into our genes. It is the essence-gene's programme – a godly programme.

Each of our incarnations is a present from God, delivered from His universal laboratory. Sent to Earth, we come to accomplish the necessary evolutionary assignments of the educational curriculum based on godly and spiritual energies.

Two essence-genes

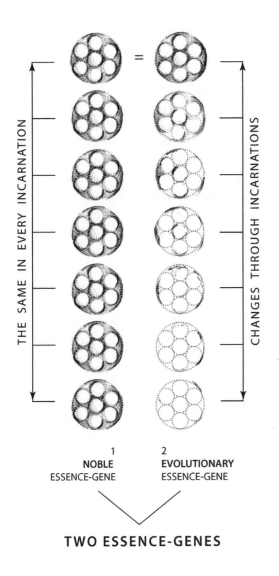

1
NOBLE
ESSENCE-GENE

2
EVOLUTIONARY
ESSENCE-GENE

TWO ESSENCE-GENES

THE SAME IN EVERY INCARNATION

CHANGES THROUGH INCARNATIONS

The evolvement of each human seed is programmed through the application of two essence-genes. One of these genes serves as a reference. It is the initial essence-gene, called the *noble gene*[32]. Regardless of the body in which it operates, this gene does not change because it is already at the level of evolutionary completion. This gene is connected to the Universal *Mechanism of Conscience*[33] and *Divine Justice*[34].

The second essence-gene is an evolutionary essence-gene; hence it is exposed to evolution through the programme of *reincarnation*[35]. Its ultimate target is to evolve the consciousness of each bodily cell to the level of cerebral consciousness, while making sure all cells become saturated with essence-energy. When this is achieved, the evolutionary essence-gene reaches the level of the initial essence-gene (noble gene). Such a human becomes a *perfect human* and is a fully integrated whole.

Each cell of a perfect human is considered a *cell-brain*[36] hence the billions of cell-genes of their body can be used to fortify the genomes of those who are yet to become perfect humans. Those gene-engraftments, by the cell-genes of the perfect humans, accelerate the evolvement of the entities who have received them.

How does it work?

A noble essence-gene continuously *emits its essence-energy*[37] throughout the dimension in which it is embodied. The entities present in that dimension who have been engrafted with the cell-genes of that noble essence-gene, benefit from those subtle energy vibrations. The more essence-energy these entities are able to receive, the faster will they evolve.

Cosmic genetic engineering[38]

The essence-genes just mentioned are not identical to what terrestrial science describes as *genes*. These essence-genes are manufactured in the Creator's workshop and, as celestial seeds, they contain energy/information of the dimension of their cosmic origin. That very energy plots our path through material realms and is the key for our evolutionary fulfilment.

The ability to receive the essence-energy, emanating from the noble essence-genes of
Moses-Jesus-Mohammed-Mevlana-Beyti-Kadri,
speeds up the evolution of people engrafted with the cell-genes of any
of these *6 noble essence-genes*[39]

The entire gene pool of humans, currently present on our planet, is the result of a celestial gene-grafting work performed in the cosmic laboratories. For example, the cell-genes of the Holy Prophets such as Moses, Jesus Christ and Mohammed, as well as the cell-genes of great minds of the past that had reached the level of a perfect human, over millennia have been used for grafting purposes – in an endeavour by the celestial realm to manifest the full potential of a human seed on a large scale. Since the evolutionary essence-gene of those prominent individuals had reached the level of their noble essence-gene, their cell-genes were suitable to be used as evolutionary accelerators.

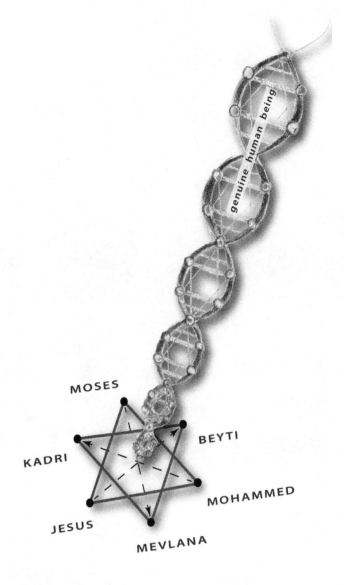

Due to this celestial laboratory work, we, humans, share a great number of the same genes. We even carry the cell-genes of the Holy Prophets. According to celestial genetic engineering, *we are all brothers and sisters*[40]. On the worldly plane though, we are yet to mirror it with our behaviour.

Through the evolvement of our evolutionary essence-gene, the universe gradually claims us back to the coordinates of its power. The *evolution of our cells*[139] is crucial to this process. Through their own awareness, our cells collaborate with the universe and eventually become immaculate transmission centres of universal energy.

Ω1 (*41) (1986)

Ω2

Ω3

Ω5 (1990)

Ω6 (1661)

Ω4

REGULAR COSMIC CURRENTS

(1992 – 2000)

(1992 – 2000)

(1992 – 2000)

K1 (*42) (1991)

K2 (1992)

Ω7 SPECIAL COSMIC CURRENTS

Ω8

Ω9

K3 (1993)

2

ENERGY
OF TIME

REGULAR COSMIC CURRENTS

NOW NOW NOW NOW NOW NOW

TIMELINE

DRIVE TOWARDS THE ESSENCE-VIBRATION

A seed sprouts, blooms and produces its fruits most effectively under the light equivalent to its own essence-vibration. Humans possess an inner drive towards that vibration. Thus we are not attracted to every book, every person, every film or every city. We read books, find friends, watch movies, or live in cities – which mostly correspond to the vibration of our essence, in a given moment in our life.

This is the reason behind some people's changing their jobs, country, or moving to another continent. Even seemingly insignificant change at work, such as getting a new boss, can trigger changes of great consequences for some employees – to the extent that they might be challenged to survive in the company's new energy setting.

> *All things have a frequency and a vibration.*
> *– Nikola Tesla.*

I have met a young woman who was thriving at her work and was happy and contented till her boss changed. The new one assessed her job performance in a different way, which triggered a low self-esteem attitude in her. She then felt unworthy, unconfident, and eventually hated going to work. The solution was in finding the power to move on, out of that company, into an energetically more suitable working environment. This person is now self-employed. She is thriving again, in an energy field vibrationally closer to the frequency of her essence-vibration.

If there is no necessity to induce change, as in the case of this young woman, the programme of curiosity will take us around different and new energy settings so that we can pick up fresh vibrations and assimilate them within our essence. We are on the task to animate the entire frequency range encoded in our essence-genes. The road is therefore long. It is a gradual process for which a seed needs lifetimes, in various energy mediums.

WEALTH FROM THE COSMIC DEPTHS

The unknown cosmic depths are firstly encountered by our thoughts. Thought therefore precedes our body in that adventure, as well as any terrestrial technological device such as rockets. For a body to access the same advanced dimensions, our crude matter constitution needs to be empowered by receiving its essence-energy (spiritual energy) – otherwise it will be destroyed. Since currently our thought can enter and sustain the energy of much higher evolutionary dimensions than our body is able to, we can consider our thought more powerful than our physical cells.

When it comes to the possibility of living in a higher evolutionary dimension, we need to evolve through particular energies first. Therefore, prior to our physical *ascension*[43] we are meticulously prepared to reach the body, consciousness and personality, required by the energy intensity and the frequency of that higher dimension.

On our evolutionary journey through the scales of energies, we reach the layers of high dimensions according to our thought power. The capacity to produce new ideas and to act creatively is also in proportion to the distance to which our thought can travel (by its frequency). The higher the energy dimension accessed by a human's thought frequency, the more original and revolutionary ideas are potentially born. However, since a premature piping into the strong energy layers would be detrimental, it is prevented by the application of the law of gradual advancement (permission, or deservance).

The brain of a creative human being has the ability to interpret, as *inspiration*[44], the subtle energy signals coming from various sources on Earth as well. Such signals can be picked up from nature or other humans, hence the variety of subjects and degrees of abstraction present in artworks.

IMPACT OF THE ENERGY OF TIME

Whatever man-made object we look at, in its energy composition there is a fusion of three awareness coordinates: *cellular awareness of the material used*[45], awareness of the artist/designer and awareness of the craftsman/builder. What also influences the final form of an artefact is the vibrational property of the collective consciousness, supplemented with the cosmic currents present on Earth at the time of that production. This planetary energy mix is regarded as time-energy (time-consciousness) and is specific to any given moment on Earth.

The fashion industry is a good example of marketing advantages gained by a frequent application of time-energy. Each new fashion line translates the latest coordinates of the collective consciousness and cosmic energy into novel forms. The fresh energy within those products hugely adds to their marketing value, and strongly appeals to a certain segment of population.

Some people, however, do not welcome changes so they do not go for the new energy epitomised in the latest product lines on the market. Those who are more inclined to go for new books,

We crave for new sensations but soon become indifferent to them. The wonders of yesterday are today common occurrences – Nikola Tesla.

films, furniture, clothes or holiday locations, grow and change with the changing time-energy on the planet. They love new energy and comfortably handle it.

A new energy does not automatically disqualify the energy of old products and their value. Obsolescence is reached gradually – only after the energy of the old is fully digested.

There are also products that have become recognised as *classics*. They are found across industries and their value withstands the challenges imposed by new energy and trends. As outstanding examples of their own kind, they might finish in museums or private collections. The new products will emerge, according to the specifics of the changing time-energy, and replace them. This is not surprising, because a new energy, which continuously reaches our planet from the depths of the universe, potentially upgrades all existing systems and designs.

"To go with the flow" would require a capacity to endure the rhythms and intensity of the time-energy.

TURNING ENERGY INTO INFORMATION AND INFORMATION INTO KNOWLEDGE

Universal information is transferred through energy particles

Information riches our planet as energy particles from celestial realms, in order to sprout seeds on Earth. However, energy becomes information relevant to us only after we decode it and consequently give it a meaning, while filtering it through our logic. That particular energy/frequency is then stored in our cerebral archive as our organic component. A *parallel record*[46] is maintained in the universal computers, on our personal diskettes, where all knowledge and consciousness we have attained through numerous lifetimes are treasured.

Deriving the information

Wherever we happen to be, our senses are bombarded with energy. Processing that energy, and deriving information from it, is a continuous job for our entire being. We draw conclusions and then act upon them, consciously or unconsciously, based on reading the energy vibrations present in our surroundings.

To draw information consciously, our full attention is required. Attention is therefore a precious currency we give in exchange for information. However, if not careful, we can needlessly spend our attention-units on trivial matters, and exhaust ourselves before we reach any relevant information.

Information, as energy, can either nest in our biology or fail to find a suitable place there. In other words, the destiny of energy we are exposed to depends on its compatibility with our personal energy field. The greater the compatibility, the higher the degree of pleasure and acceptance – pertaining to the perception of a particular energy.

Biologically archived frequencies

Information derived from various energy vibrations turns into knowledge when we comprehend its meaning, absorb its frequency/ energy and are able to apply that information, in a positive way, to the betterment of society. Knowledge therefore represents biologically archived scales of frequencies that we can consciously and positively operate from.

Our planetary knowledge is a minute sample of frequencies present in the vastness of creation. Each drop of that knowledge has been earned through the great efforts of brain energies. Nikola Tesla revealed how it used to

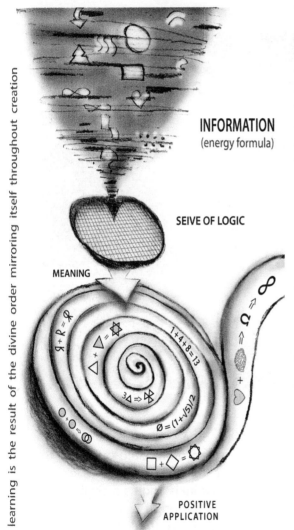

INFORMATION
(energy formula)

SEIVE OF LOGIC

MEANING

POSITIVE
APPLICATION

KNOWLEDGE

learning is the result of the divine order mirroring itself throughout creation

31

take him days, weeks and even months, to intensify his mental concentration in order to get rid of old impressions and wishes – and so to fill his mind with new themes, in line with the project he wished to work on. Throughout years of rigorous self-training, the command he acquired over his brain energies made his focus and his willpower truly exceptional. Hence the sheer number and significance of the innovations Tesla bestowed on our planet is yet to be matched by another human brain.

> *When I get a new idea, I start at once building it up in my imagination, and make improvements and operate the device in my mind. When I have gone so far as to embody everything in my invention, every possible improvement I can think of, and when I see no fault anywhere, I put into concrete form the final product of my brain. – Nikola Tesla*

Our thought is a space traveller. The greater its power and faster its speed are, the further the distances and the dimensions it can reach.

$1+1=2$

$1+1 \neq 2^{(*47)}$

Upgrading the knowledge

Energy is in constant flow and interaction. As we accommodate ourselves to those fluctuations and to the frequency of higher dimensions, we evolve and upgrade our knowledge accordingly – both as individuals and as a civilisation. Hence knowledge is not a fixed category. For that reason, it is quite possible that one day we will encounter findings that are even contradictory to some well-established scientific principles on our planet; such as *speed of light* being constant.

I learned a dozen languages, studied literature and arts, spent my best years in libraries reading everything that came my way, and though I sometimes felt I was losing time, I quickly realized it was the best thing I ever did. – Nikola Tesla

Each passing day ushers in new and stronger energies on Earth, which prepare the life-medium on it for future centuries. To keep up with the cosmic curriculum, the implementation of new energies is therefore a (life) imperative. This upgrading of our knowledge-continuum, with new frequencies, naturally makes some knowledge obsolete. However, the importance of the old is indisputable because the old is always an energy-base to the new. Thus we climb the stairs of energies, and construct our life-style upon the knowledge and consciousness attained through experiencing those energy steps.

However, knowledge and learning, as we practise it, is of a temporary significance to the evolving (conscious) energy that we epitomise. In more advanced dimensions far away from matter, where the medium of energy particles becomes exhausted, both knowledge and learning terminate and life becomes propagated through different modalities. This can also be understood as the accomplishment of learning within one infinity. Moving on to a new infinity will present new laws and ways to existence – all within another set of objectives and boundaries.

An infinite number of infinities within an all-encompassing infinity is a brain-wracking "paradox" of the Absolute Singularity. To illustrate the viability of this organisational pattern the geometries called *fractals*, widely found in nature, can help us. If we look at the fascinating structure of a *romanesco cauliflower*, we notice that each of its conical segments, regardless of its size or position, resembles the shape of the entire cauliflower. By exhibiting a pattern of endless propagation through self-alike fragments, this example, taken from the vegetable garden, shows an infinite potential of evolvement within a finite material form.

The human being is an energy system that appears confined by a physical body, yet human awareness and consciousness are subject to infinite expansion.

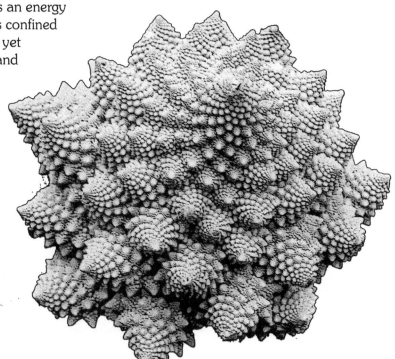

Through an astonishing order and structural beauty, the romanesco cauliflower reminds us that every point within creation is the beginning of a new infinity

the sound frequency of the atomic whole is carried by the number 7 (*49)

7 x 7 – ATOMIC WHOLE

atomic bond (*48)

7

Transfer of knowledge is transfer of energy

Knowledge acquired on Earth in its essence is of the celestial origin, and indicates the evolutionary level of our civilisation.

The power of our brain is crucial in catapulting our thought into the energy layers beyond this planet, where thought can knock on the doors of various higher dimensions. If thought frequency is sufficient to open those doors, it can bring back some souvenirs from those encounters. According to his level of consciousness, the individual then interprets that energy/information and blends it with existing knowledge.

Vibrations of cosmic sounds, light, the Sun, the Moon, of each entity in the starry sky, reach our planet. They are sources of information. However, we are still unable to understand their language, because there is a scale of frequencies and meanings between us and them that we have to conquer first. In other words, we can only decode as much of the energy available on Earth as our evolutionary level allows.

The Earth's magnetic field represents a blend of cosmic influences and energy emanations of the mineral, plant, animal and human world. We derive information from that field, parallel to our perception. Nikola Tesla emphasised the quality of perception, as an important element in the forming of ideas and opinions. According to him, fragmentary perception is responsible for many mad ideas and illnesses – even though our body has the capacity to receive influences in a full enough scope to reach the truth.

The mechanism of receiving a frequency, assimilating it and later on sharing it as information/knowledge, functions on many levels – such as on the level of individuals, ethnic groups or states. The energy exchanges within each level and between different levels, contribute to the propagating of knowledge and reaching the truth. The more parties come to the same conclusions, the faster those conclusions become accepted as truth. Consequently, a frequency adjustment amongst different parties takes place and the programme of unification proceeds thus.

Fundamentally, both frequency adjustment and unification are of a cosmic scope.

THE BRAIN IS A COSMIC COMPUTER

Human's brain power leads our civilisation

The *human brain*[140] is present at the terrestrial dimension, yet it is activated and powered by energies attracted from puzzling cosmic depths. (Fontanelles, the soft spots between the bony plates of a baby's skull, are open until the baby's brain attains power to attract cosmic energy on its own). Our brain connects us to the universal medium, and to the Mechanism of Equilibrium in nature. It is a telex-like apparatus, which also decodes various signals received from our body and our worldly environment.

Thought is like an arrow, able to reach faraway celestial strata. As a result of such encounters, our thought brings down and emits a new energy/information to fortify the world. The outcome of this capacity is evident through theories, stories, visions, revelations, discoveries, innovations, and art, which humans offer to their society. Thus, parallel to our thought power, we continuously weave new frequencies into the tapestry of terrestrial knowledge and collective consciousness. The scientific, technological and social development of our civilisation is a direct result of the power of the human brain.

All information ever given to our planet is to help human beings understand the supremacy of the Divine Plan and consequently, as genetically fulfilled individuals, choose to serve it.

The decoding of the signals received by the brain depends on the brain's perceptive power and the thought frequency.

Hence people of a different consciousness and evolutionary level, derive different information even from the same source.

The progressive development of man is vitally dependent on invention. It is the most important product of his creative brain. Its ultimate purpose is the complete mastery of mind over the material world, the harnessing of the forces of nature to human needs.
– Nikola Tesla

A moving threshold

Our brain is the storehouse of all the knowledge we have ever acquired. The light of that knowledge is precious, even for our surrounding. For that reason, learning has always been an important factor in the evolution of humanity and in the expansion of its consciousness. Moving towards the higher dimensions therefore relies on the energies we attract by our brain. Since much depends on the power of this organ, how do we stimulate it?

We enlarge our brain's capacity by our cerebral efforts. As we deal with the energy/information unknown to us, grows the volume of energies our thought can operate through. The stronger the energy of the information source, the more vigorous the brain's exercise is – hence the speed of our thought increases as well.

Attracting energy/information from the dimensions beyond our planet by our brain, in proportion to the power of our brain energies, is not a new phenomenon on the evolutionary chart of humans. However, as we evolve, by climbing the evolutionary dimensions, the energy thresholds required to be reached also ascend.

We are *biological computers*[50] unfolding the programmes, we have been placed into by the might of our Designer! In comparison to the computers we have developed on Earth, we, human-computers, can feel – based on how we perceive, select and process both inner and outside signals.

THOUGHT PRECEDES CREATION

Whatever man-made objects we see around us, at one stage they were thoughts in the *mind*[141] of the human who conceived them. If we consistently apply that same principle, it would mean that even we ourselves, and what we call *nature*, would have firstly been a thought in a Cosmic Brain.

The Cosmic Brain seems to be utilising the principle of *harmonic economy*: viable models are applied throughout the innumerable levels, both as operational ordinances and as the structural pattern of the physical forms – from tiny to mega systems.

The entire creation is brought into existence, organised and supervised through the same laws hence the essence of the universe and the essence of a human are based on common properties. To learn the secret of who we are, by reaching our essence, would therefore unlock the *secrets of the universe*[51].

Thought is a bridge. It keeps us connected to the celestial realm, which is our prime life-source. Thus gymnastics for the brain is the most preferable exercise for each human being.

Brain power can be seen as a volume that stretches according to the power of our thought. It grows parallel to our capacity to reach and decode the energies of advanced dimensions beyond Earth. However, since we have not yet attained the level of our full genetic potential, at our current stage of evolvement our thought is still undergoing intensive training. The main source of the evolutionary challenges and tests for our thought come from the special cosmic energy, directed towards our planet, and from our encounters with other humans.

THOUGHT – AN ANTI-MATTER TRANSMITTER

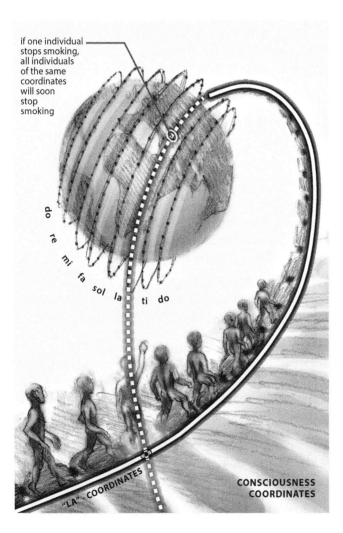

if one individual stops smoking, all individuals of the same coordinates will soon stop smoking

do
re
mi
fa
sol la ti do

"LA" COORDINATES

CONSCIOUSNESS COORDINATES

Conveyance of an invisible energy

Thought[52] is a function of energy unknown to us. It is an invisible pathway of the Power that is instrumental in bringing everything into existence. The significance of this Power has been indicated by the well-known Biblical sentence: "And God said, *Let there be light: and there was light.*" (Genesis 1:3)

All sacred books informed us that GOD had *Thought things into existence.* God conceived a meaning and instilled it into His words. The realms of spirit and matter were therefore bridged by the power of meaning and intent. *But his command, When He intendeth a thing, is only that He saith unto it: "Be!"* – *And it is.* [Koran (36:82)].

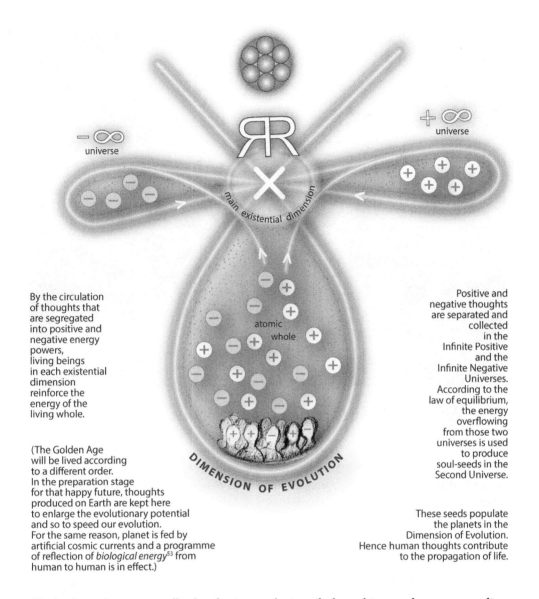

By the circulation of thoughts that are segregated into positive and negative energy powers, living beings in each existential dimension reinforce the energy of the living whole.

(The Golden Age will be lived according to a different order. In the preparation stage for that happy future, thoughts produced on Earth are kept here to enlarge the evolutionary potential and so to speed our evolution. For the same reason, planet is fed by artificial cosmic currents and a programme of reflection of *biological energy*[53] from human to human is in effect.)

Positive and negative thoughts are separated and collected in the Infinite Positive and the Infinite Negative Universes. According to the law of equilibrium, the energy overflowing from those two universes is used to produce soul-seeds in the Second Universe.

These seeds populate the planets in the Dimension of Evolution. Hence human thoughts contribute to the propagation of life.

Each thought potentially leads to a chain of thoughts, and corresponding manifestations. The amassing of thoughts creates a magnetic field.

No thought is ever lost. A record of them all, as well as of all speech that has ever been uttered, is present in the universal storehouses. So-called *Positive and Negative Infinite Universes*[54] treasure positive and negative thoughts. These thoughts originate from the entire Atomic Whole. The two Infinte Universes are in a state of mutual equilibrium, and are a source fundamental in producing soul-seeds. Created in the Main Existential Dimension, the soul-seeds are sent to the Dimension of Evolution, within the realms of space and time, to advance through necessary energy spectrums[*]. Hence new human lives and new worlds emerge from our thought potential and, consequently, universes come into being from the energy behind our recycled thoughts. (*the illustration, page 20)

The Words of God increase our thought frequency

Humans evolve by the influences they exert on one another, as individuals and as social groups. Thoughts are one of those influences, albeit their impact is not always obvious. Collective consciousness is a magnetic field composed of the frequencies pertaining to science, religion, art and learning, which a society lives on. This energy field is indicative of the evolutionary level of each culture.

Besides being susceptible to the thoughts of those around us in our terrestrial environment, for millennia our thoughts have been under the influence of what is commonly referred to as the *Words of God*, delivered to our planet through celestial reflection mechanisms. The *Far East Philosophies* and the sacred books have been purifying and training us through their energy and, over the centuries, our thought frequencies and our mental potential have been increasing. The resonances of their letter and sound frequencies have been appropriating us to the divine light, by causing gradual alterations in our consciousness.

Even though the *sacred books are celestial scripts*[55] packed with celestial information, the physical and administrative aspects of the celestial hierarchy have been concealed or just metaphorically hinted at in them – because centuries ago we were not ready for explicit universal information and truth. However, most importantly, these books have been conveying to us the energies of the evolutionary dimensions they have come from.

Written thought

There is a plane of existence where energy, currently operating through a human being, will transcend the need for books. If we look at the young generation on Earth, we can see such a tendency. They appear less inclined to read. The energy of the past, captured in the works of literary giants such as Hugo, Dickens or Shakespeare, seems far less meaningful to them than to their parents; as if the frequencies found in those books, and the books in general, are rather irrelevant to young generation. On the other hand, these new kids are much attracted to the sources of information with a fast flow of data on multiple platforms. Hence the use of computer technology makes them feel like a fish in water.

As a communication method, writing is used in the lower evolvement dimensions of humanity. It has been introduced to our planet as an additional way for personal expression, because we were not able to communicate telepathically – in other words, due to an insufficient evolvement of the human brain at the time.

Even though millennia have passed since the appearance of the first alphabets on Earth, our brain is still not able to communicate directly with other humans or with beings from the animal and plant worlds. If we are to become one with creation, we must therefore empower and refine ourselves further. In some way, the brains of the young on Earth might be more developed than ours, hence their immediate affiliation with high technology and disinterest in reading books. They might even struggle to adjust to the archaic speed of the thoughts of the adults around them. The generation clash has never been easy to deal with. Despite the challenges, it leads to a shift in consciousness of both sides. Love eases and accelerates that process.

Our thought speed can surpass the speed of light

Human thought is a space traveller. As a result of this intangible brain activity, we have already made numerous intergalactic connections. Those encounters, which we are not even aware of, are an evolutionary necessity. They broaden the spectrum of energies we can operate through and so prepare us for our future, in the realities beyond the evolutionary dimension of Earth.

Our brain energies are on a constant assignment to reach the stage where they can directly work with energy from the Universal dimension. They will ultimately take full control over the process of thinking and be able to operate beyond the frequency of thought. Meditation is helpful in that direction, though it is not the sole factor to take us to those evolvement heights.

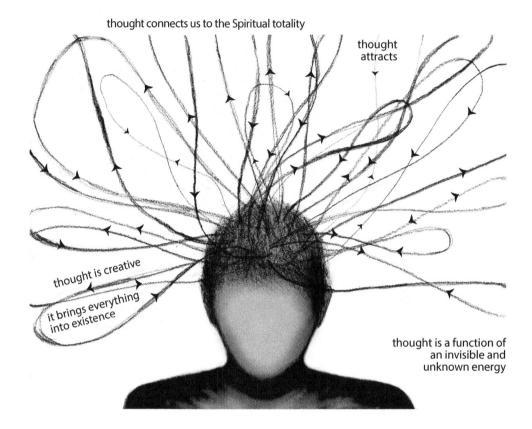

thought connects us to the Spiritual totality

thought attracts

thought is creative

it brings everything into existence

thought is a function of an invisible and unknown energy

Keeping our thoughts at a stable frequency, affects our health in a positive way. On the other hand, interfering with others by obstructing their thought frequency, due to our inability to maintain a harmonious interaction, directly affects the health of both parties in a negative way.

There is a correlation between the speed of our thought and the *speed of light*. When we enter the life-medium of the 3rd Evolutionary dimension on Earth, the frequency of our thought corresponds to the *speed of light*[56]. As we evolve, and reach the evolutionary stages beyond the 3rd Evolutionary dimension, our thought speed increases and surpasses the *speed of light*. It means that our thought can reach distances beyond the volume where light travels at a speed of 300,000 km per second.

Beyond this boundary, the measurements of time used on Earth are not valid and the domain of *light-years*[57] begins.

When our brain energy transcends *light-years*, it will gradually take all lights under its supervision. Hence through our brain power, we will be able to create universes and administer them as masters of the orders we will establish there. Those creations will inevitably comply with the universal laws since ego does not exist in advanced realities.

Dimension of *ABSOLUTE TIME*[58] – Dimension of Nothingness
(Divine Order – Almighty The Absolute)

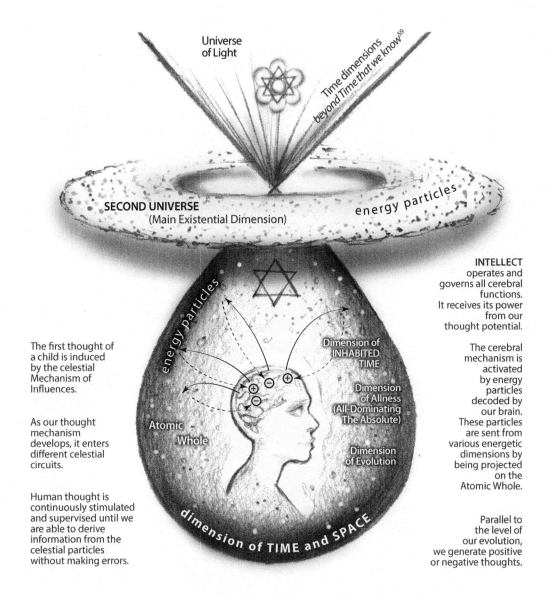

Universe
of Light

Time dimensions
beyond Time that we know[59]

SECOND UNIVERSE
(Main Existential Dimension)

energy particles

energy particles

Dimension of
INHABITED
TIME

Dimension
of Allness
(All-Dominating
The Absolute)

Dimension
of Evolution

Atomic
Whole

dimension of TIME and SPACE

The first thought of
a child is induced
by the celestial
Mechanism of
Influences.

As our thought
mechanism
develops, it enters
different celestial
circuits.

Human thought is
continuously stimulated
and supervised until we
are able to derive
information from the
celestial particles
without making errors.

INTELLECT
operates and
governs all cerebral
functions.
It receives its power
from our
thought potential.

The cerebral
mechanism is
activated
by energy
particles
decoded by
our brain.
These particles
are sent from
various energetic
dimensions by
being projected
on the
Atomic Whole.

Parallel to
the level of
our evolution,
we generate positive
or negative thoughts.

Human brains project the godly and universal orders onto their own living medium

*In no way can we get such an overwhelming idea of the grandeur of Nature than
when we consider, that in accordance with the law of the conservation of energy,
throughout the Infinite, the forces are in a perfect balance, and hence the energy of
a single thought may determine the motion of a Universe. – Nikola Tesla*

The capacity
to project our
brain energy to
operate beyond the
light-year boundary,
currently sounds like a
wild fantasy since a *light-
year* is a distance of just under
10 trillion kilometres. However,
this achievement is only one of the
thresholds on our evolutionary trajectory.

Even though, at the moment, we are still
experiencing the stages of an imperfect terrestrial
human, we are truly cosmic beings who are trained to
return to their cosmic homeland. We are genuinely heading towards
the stars that our inner child has never stopped dreaming about! Only in those
mediums would the potential of our essence-energy fully unfold.

Our thought opens those supreme pathways for our body to follow. The brain is
therefore instrumental in manifesting our cosmic potential and destiny.

Kürz 2 (*42)
(dimnsion of truth)

Beta Nova 60

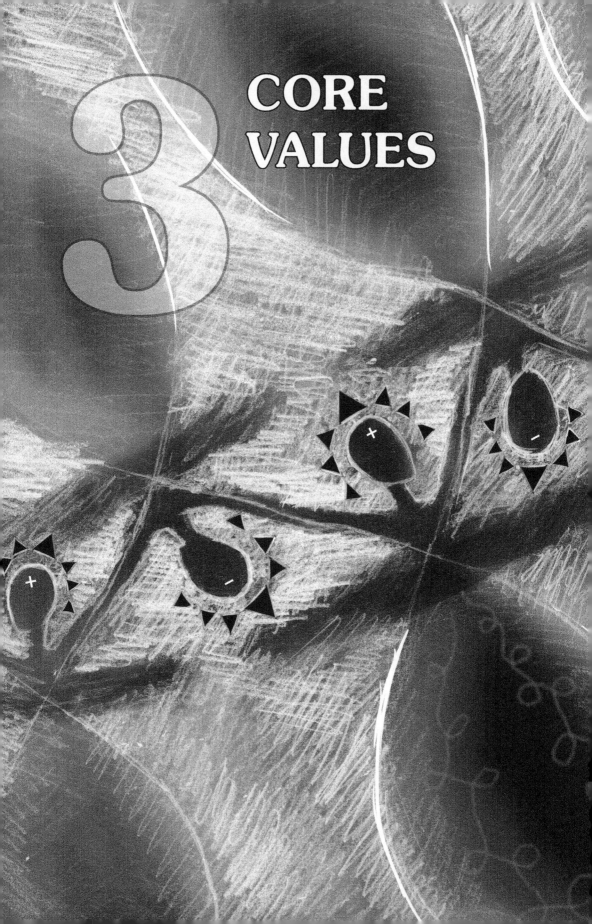

3 CORE VALUES

We are godly seeds. The essence-properties of the godly personality are inherent in us and represent our ultimate potential. In order to manifest that potential, there is a need for our inner purification and evolvement.

Before we discover that the godly personality is our genetic heritage and start making conscious efforts to reach it, we put a great deal of effort into employing other behavioural patterns. Dormant, our essence-seed's properties thus wait for our spiritual awakening, which will take us beyond the manners adopted by an inert mind. Various conditionings then start to melt away, and our essence-personality progressively emerges.

According to Aristotle and Plato, the four most desirable character traits are wisdom, justice, courage and temperance. These four *cardinal virtues* were later complemented by hope, faith and charity (love) by a theological community that named those additional three as the *theological virtues*. This particular set of seven virtues was a very popular topic of discussion throughout the Middle Ages. However, since we have not mastered this old subject, which is also a leitmotiv of all sacred books, in the cosmic school on Earth we still study the same lesson – *on Virtues*.

The list of noble human qualities is very long and each one of those qualities is carried by a particular frequency. They are the priceless assets of our essence, but unless we discipline our *ego*[61], they will remain in its shadow.

PATIENCE

Patience requires a profound trust that the flow of life is a reflection of the universal laws on every situation. Patient people therefore take each event as divinely needed. They understand how obstructing the flow, by impatient behaviour, brings new elements into the picture, which takes particular development outside the divine flow. Thus instead of waiting in calm belief, and so receiving what we have to according to the divine schedule – due to our impatience, we unconsciously and gradually impact on our life's direction. Later, we might wonder why things have not unfolded to our advantage even though we actively "supported" our preferences.

Life is a highly organised structure, directed by the absolute laws of the Creator. It is to our advantage to recognise these laws and to learn to harmonise with them – rather than to ignore or bend them, in order to "suit" each of our desires and expectations. In any case, we cannot deviate from the absolute laws – they are in application, as independent of any law we make on Earth. The bigger the discrepancy between these two sets of laws, the less evolved we are as a civilisation and the more uncomfortable we feel while living on Earth. No lasting happiness will transpire until the divine laws are fully understood and followed.

In familiarising ourselves with these laws, at one point in our evolution we will be led to realise that, regardless of our efforts, nothing will ever happen until the time for it is right. Forcing things into being by not having enough patience, works against the laws of life and so against us.

Patience is the nobility of a relaxed mind that has accepted life as it is. Such an individual would not waste energy on impatient objections or action, but would gracefully value their personal position in every situation. Such an attitude will be energising – contrary to impatience, which is energy draining.

Patience implies tolerance.

TOLERANCE

A tolerant person is much in control of their behaviour.

Similar to patience, tolerance requires acceptance of the evolutionary stage of each individual on the planet, and acceptance of the sequence of events in our life regardless of how challenging their outcome might be. We are to tolerate literally everything, and in an equal manner, because all experiences are the result of the same universal laws.

However, tolerance is not passivity or resignation. It comes from an ability to give space to others and to refrain from imposing personal expectations on them. A tolerant person is capable of forgiving and supporting others, wherever these others are in their evolution.

A tolerant person is positive and respectful in all circumstances.

RESPECT

Respect is not a mental property but rather esteem expressed through action. Starting from the self, respect extends to all humans, and all aspects of civilisation and nature. Without self-respect it is unlikely that one will be able to show honest respect of any kind.

Lots of troubles on our planet, such as crime, wars or exploitation, originate from the lack of this virtue.

An individual, who respects another person, demonstrates their respect for the Creator at the same time. At a certain stage of our evolution, we even start respecting the tiniest particle in existence, as well as the entire creation – known or unknown to us. For, we understand that each particle epitomises the pre-eminence of the Creator. This is a worshipping of the Creator through our consciousness, and signifies the concluding stage of worshipping.

True respect is based on appreciation, not on fear or interest. It flourishes on mere gratitude for having a place in God's existential orders. A person, whose respect is of this scope, is humble enough to love everything and everyone.

Respect is in the foundation of morality and any correct behaviour. We invite respect if we are tolerant, patient and loving. To embed respect in a relationship, or organisation, can take time – though all that has been built up can crumble in an instant due to a single thoughtless deed.

The more respectful a person is, the more responsible they are.

RESPONSIBILITY

Responsibility is a virtue that is highly important when a person goes into communication or any collaboration with others. It is hard to achieve much, if the degree of responsibility differs a lot between the parties involved.

When we appreciate our own time, we also respect the time of other people so we do everything to prevent the wasting of anyone's time. The responsibility an individual undertakes in social interactions is therefore parallel to the responsibility they have for their own thoughts, words and behaviour.

If we treat our given word as law, it means we are responsible for our behaviour and appreciate others at the same time. A lack of responsibility indicates insufficient self-awareness, self-respect and willpower – besides demonstrating disregard for other people.

In order to step into an evolvement through the energy of the Universal dimension, responsibility is one of the crucial virtues – though, we need to complete our evolvement through the Religious dimension first.

Living in advanced dimensions requires discipline in undertaking a service, a conscious mission, within the order of the universe. In those dimensions, it would be too risky to rely on people whose virtue of responsibility is insufficiently evolved, hence the gates of advanced dimensions will remain closed to them.

Without a strong sense of responsibility, a person cannot activate mission-consciousness. Mission-consciousness, exercised through the application of religious teachings, is heavily coloured by a fear of God. However, the universal mission is performed from a different consciousness level and is carried out without fear.

ACCEPTANCE

Our unconditional acceptance of other individuals and an essence-desire to serve humanity, are the topmost qualities we achieve through the evolution of our persona. These qualities are essential to all integration processes.

In order to accept something, one often needs to employ blind faith – hence faith has been a pivotal virtue, which the sacred books have tried to develop in us.

During the training through the Religious dimension, people became accustomed to their prayers being fulfilled. By recognising a metaphysical Power that would answer their prayers, they were lead to develop their belief in God. However, after this stage, a different programme comes into effect: humans are tested as to whether they accept God and His creation, even in the face of unpleasant situations or when things go contrary to what they would wish. In other words, individuals who have completed their evolution through the Religious dimension are then tested so that it becomes clear whether they accepted God due to their self-interest (because God was fulfilling their prayers), or due to a genuine recognition of the sovereignty of God and His orders. This second stage of our divine training is the evolution through the Universal dimension – where we are continuously tested through our interaction with others, and by unexpected and unpleasant events. At this level of evolution we learn truth by facing the opposites, and so the solidity of our faith is thoroughly challenged.

Differences between people originate from the degrees of both their evolvement and completion of their karma. They are evident through people's varied consciousness levels and capacities to absorb divine light. That is normal, and so it is to be accepted and lovingly tolerated. Even though some people can attract only a millionth part of the special cosmic currents, which shower the planet to accelerate the evolution of all life on it, each human on Earth has been permitted to evolve here right now – with the rest of the 7 billion people given the same opportunity. This opportunity is for the betterment of individuals, society and this planet since it complies with the *Lordly Orders*[62] pertaining to evolution on Earth. Therefore, it is not due to "chance" but is in line with the evolutionary plan that all of us, currently living on this planet, are equally welcome and appreciated.

Unfortunately, people discriminate through views on skin colour, religious and other beliefs. Differences in sexual, food or dressing preferences are still seen as a reason to reject other individuals and thus to maintain an unhealthy distance towards some people or cultures.

Stopping the flow of the essence-energy between humans, due to not accepting the differences between us, is highly inappropriate and hinders our evolution.

We keep forgetting that it is only due to our limited perception and conditioned belief that we appear separated; but we are like the fingers of a hand – though different, each one has a specific and indispensable role that supports our common purpose.

COMPASSION

Compassion is the sensibility of an individual who understands another person's state of being and, by mirroring it inside themselves, offers constructive support. The help might be a seemingly simple act – such as a smile, willingness to listen, a kind word, or other caring gestures.

Compassion is also empathy for the sufferings of all living beings. A compassionate person has stepped out of their individualistic views and obsessions with the self. It does not automatically mean that those people have neglected themselves. On the contrary, only by knowing how to care about our own self first, can we exercise a caring behaviour in our interactions with others.

A compassionate person will find a way to notice those who need compassion, and find the time to be beside them.

Compassion is an expression of selfless love.

> *Though free to think and act, we are held together, like the stars in the firmament, with ties inseparable. These ties cannot be seen, but we can feel them. I cut myself in the finger, and it pains me: this finger is a part of me. I see a friend hurt, and it hurts me, too: my friend and I are one. – Nikola Tesla*

LOVE

Love dissolves boundaries

Love is a powerful vibration[63] that leads us into our essence, by melting all obstacles and opening all doors on that way. There is no power to triumph over love.

Love is fundamental to our unconditional acceptance of the entire creation, since love does not make any discrimination. It is a vibration compatible with everything in life. Hence, at the level of universal love, an individual embraces all in an equal manner. Even microbes or parasites are appreciated to the same degree as the most beautiful butterfly or a beloved pet.

Love is experienced parallel to the *frequency*[64] of an individual

Owing to the dimensional frequency of our planet, love commonly experienced here is still inferior to the unconditional-conscious-universal love, and is therefore subject to evolvement. It is on the way to firstly transcend the frequencies of sexual love and then reach divine love.

To speed up this particular progress and ease the load of negativities present on Earth, the whole planet has been exposed to *supplementation with the frequency of universal love*[65] from the celestial realm. The capacity to receive these frequencies depends on the evolutionary level of each person. People of a higher evolvement, utilise these cosmic influences through philanthropic love and acceptance. Some others though might go for adultery, which is their way of interpreting those powerful frequencies.

Attraction power

Love is an all-encompassing, powerful vibration of the divine waves that has manifested life. It holds the countless dimensions together – from the tiny to the mega atomic wholes of the existential systems. This vibration is built into our genetic material. Owing to the attraction power inherent in love, love is the strongest bonding element amongst people and is able to endure all separation.

The power of attraction emerged at the early stages of the *energy formation processes*[66] and is integral to all four fundamental forces of nature so far known to our science (gravity, electromagnetism, then strong and weak nuclear force). Any action of any of these four major forces therefore involves the power of attraction, which means that the whole of nature and life thrive on the power of attraction.

The manifestation of form-energy (an intensified energy recognised as crude matter) is also a result of the transformation processes that involve the power of attraction. Through those routes, various energies were fertilised and universes came into existence.

Attraction is instrumental in spiritualising our crude-matter body. Thought plays a great part in that process, because it is via thought that our material body communicates with the celestial realms of light.

Thought itself possesses an immense attraction power. For example, if we intensively think of somebody who is not friendly with us, our thoughts will attract the negative energy of such a person and place it in our aura. Owing to the impact of that negative energy, we will not be able to experience ourselves authentically. Control over our thoughts is therefore immeasurably important.

When it comes to the need of our cells to directly draw necessary cosmic energy, again, the power of attraction is critical to that process. The quantity of attracted energies received, depends on the awareness level of each cell.

The realms of light and matter are bridged by thought due to its attraction power. The vibrations of love maintain that connection. They keep light and matter together in an atomic whole. Each human is proof of this order.

Universal love (unconditional love) is a conscious love

Universal love is not governed by feelings since feelings originate from our desires. This love is disciplined by logic. Love based on emotions/sentiment/romantic visions only, is not love that is free from expectations (sometimes mindless ones); hence is destined for disappointments. Such love is a roller coaster that can develop mind-blowing momentum and heights – yet, in an instant, it can take us down with the same overwhelming intensity.

People immersed in the vibration of universal love do not depend on whether somebody loves them or not, and they act beyond sentiment. At that stage, a person does not even feel a need to utter the word *love*, or talk about love, because she or he has become one with it. Hence this love is expressed through deeds, rather than words.

In conscious love, there are no ups and downs. There is only a stable unconditional embrace of the entire creation by one's free and conscious choice. Energies on all evolvement levels are going through necessary evolution, in order to reach unconditional love and thus to embrace the Total.

The more we love, the more the Essence-Power-field, called *Creator* or *God*, opens to us; and we step deeper into that field. Our frequency of love is therefore decisive in our experience of God.

Love of our cells

Nature speaks to us through the language of universal love. As a part of nature, our cells usually emanate more love to us than we consciously return to them.

Do we pay enough attention to food, feelings or thoughts, which all affect our body? Are we aware how great a companion our body is, and do we find time to keep it fit?

The human body works ceaselessly and loyally in order to enable necessary terrestrial experiences. Those experiences evolve the energy that uses our body. At the same time, the spiritualising of our crude-matter aspects takes place. This evolutionary process can be supported by correct attitudes. Unfortunately, people do not care much about the ultimate objectives of their evolution. Hence going for the experiences of worldly pleasures is usually more attractive to them than caring about a precious friend – their own body.

Changing of an era

Without love, we would not thrive and would not even come into existence. A mother's love for her child is unconditional, and is one of the highest frequencies of love on Earth. From this point of view, mothers are the most godlike beings on the planet. The very first food a child gets is the frequency of mother's love – not milk. This has been programmed by the Creator, to best suit the purpose of perpetuating the human race.

Though love is essential for our emergence and survival, its vibration is not sufficient to develop our consciousness. Thus, to the foundation made of love, reinforced by the energy of the celestial books, we need to add the frequencies of universal knowledge in order to complete our evolution.

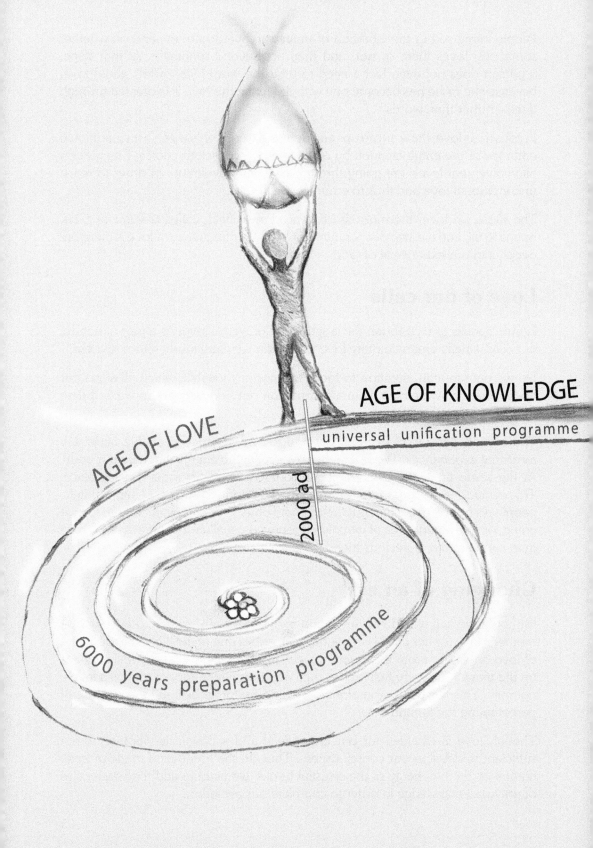

AGE OF KNOWLEDGE

AGE OF LOVE

universal unification programme

2000 ad

6000 years preparation programme

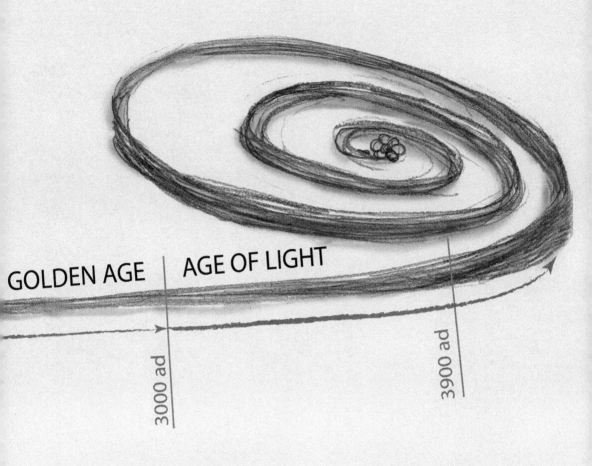

GOLDEN AGE | AGE OF LIGHT

3000 ad

3900 ad

According to the universal schedule of humans' evolution on Earth, in the year 2000, our planet officially ended the *Age of Love* (godly, religious, evolution through alpha energy) and entered the *Age of Knowledge* (universal evolution through spiritual energies – beta energy from the *Omega dimension*[67]). It is therefore a matter of evolutionary timing for people to discipline their emotional body now, by the use of logic and intellect, and shift towards the heights of universal love. Such is the path of love leading us to the essence-consciousness.

4 LEARNING THROUGH OPPOSITES

ARROGANCE
DISOBEDIENCE
CONDITIONINGS
PASSIONS
NEGATIVITIES
EGO
UNFAITHFULNESS
FEARS
JUDGEMENTALISM
TERRESTRIAL CONSCIOUSNESS
ATTACHMENTS
SUPERIORITY

FEARS

Facing the uncertainties

The initial function of fear is to protect us from going blindly into new situations. However, it is a measure of maturity when we tame this instinct and liberate ourselves from useless fears that stop our personal development.

All of us have experienced a lack of confidence in our ability to handle some situations. The uncertain outcome of those situations makes us feel apprehensive beforehand. Hence we fear that we might be unsuccessful, rejected and then embarrassed or even hurt. Giving priority to such an imagined scenario, unfortunately, can inhibit our progress since it leads to the postponement of valuable experiences.

What could help us to outgrow this mental pattern, and prepare us to successfully deal with the possible consequences that we hesitate to face? – An understanding that all experiences are equally valuable would be of the utmost benefit. Broadening the scope of observation, as well as the use of common sense, is also valuable. If we manage to step into the situations we fear, we will embark on learning instead of dwelling in assumptions.

In combating our fears, it might also be useful to ask ourselves whether (and how) we survived all the challenges that have come our way. Evidently, we are still functioning on Earth so the answer would be positive. This retrospection could remind us that the life-force, working through us, is stronger than the energy behind any "failure" or fear? Even the gloomiest circumstances, actually, support us in the direction of our most urgently needed transformations – wherever we are on our evolutionary trajectory.

In the infinities of the single existing Totality, all the constituents influence one another. This ceaseless network of interactions facilitates change and growth, on both the micro and macro levels. Therefore, to resist the unknown, and resist change, opposes the fundamental processes of life and its innate self-propagation mechanism.

In response to the conditions of their medium, energies undergo a chain of transformations. During that process, they recurrently reach the stages of saturation. Each saturation level generates a qualitative change and so mutation takes place. The energy, which operates through a human, follows the same order and advances towards its higher expressions. Gradually, it transmutes the lower vibrational states (known as our weaknesses) so that the level of the perfect human being can be achieved.

If we drop all our expectations, even of being loved and being successful, perhaps there is then nothing to fear. Experiences will surely unfold in one of two ways – pleasant or unpleasant, and in each instance there will be much to learn. It means we cannot but benefit from personal experiences.

Even those experiences that we fear the most, refresh us with their energy. With the quintessence of each experience we have an opportunity to refine our personality, and top-up some low-vibrational energy pockets within our mind-body-spirit constitution.

Personal experiences are also a testing arena for our awareness and views, and a precious catalysts in reaching the truth.

Our consciousness thrives on our experiences.

Penetrating the unknown

Living is a continuous flow of experiences. They transpire to take us from one evolvement level to another.

Every experience presents us with new energies. We gradually get used to those energies, learn to harmonise with them and eventually assimilate them through our physical and spiritual constitutions.

Each one of us has a personal homework here on Earth, related to the portion of new energy we need to attract and absorb. These energies are our stairways towards the manifestation of our full genetic potential, and they shed light on our path.

Since fears paralyse our actions and disconnect us from the divine flow of energy, succumbing to them slows our inner progress. In other words, our fear impairs the revitalisation of our cells through life-energy. A prolonged deprivation of this kind disturbs our cells' regeneration processes and is damaging to our health.

How to deal with our fears?

It can take time, and even lifetimes, to notice that our fears loyally follow us. It is only the circumstances, which provoke a particular fear, that change but our inclination to act on the basis of that fear does not change. This pattern will last till eventually we build a capacity to surrender to all our fears.

The more we accept the flow of events and trust in the perfection of the *Divine Order*[68], the less challenging it will be to face our fears. When we become capable of seeing our fears as our personal mental construct, fears will slowly lose their power over us.

We can transcend our fears not by saying *I am not afraid*, but by embracing the unknown with less and less hesitation.

ATTACHMENTS

Everything on this planet, even beauty, is arranged to test us, to seduce us into the terrestrial lifestyle of an unending desire to consume pleasures. Yes, we certainly have come to this planet to experience and saturate ourselves with terrestrial things. However, little are we aware that our passions, as well as our worldly and religious attachments, can become obstacles to our evolvement and can delay our reaching of the more advanced dimensions.

After conquering our passions, superstitions and attachments, we find ourselves at the point where we feel the same whether our wishes come true or not – because we have stopped being slaves to our own desires.

Terrestrial tests

> *Our virtues and our failings are inseparable, like force and matter.* – Nikola Tesla

Terrestrial tests are seemingly endless, since every single situation is created to test our response to the energies involved. Hence, our ability to control our thoughts, words and actions, in a given energy setup, exposes our spiritual maturity. Our behaviour is the direct result of our capacity to manage all those personality aspects, and is the truest indicator of our evolutionary level. Amongst the toughest terrestrial tests are the ones related to intoxicants, money, material goods and sex.

Excessive use of alcohol, cigarettes, drugs or even food, blocks our ability to receive cosmic energy and so deprives us from vital evolutionary nourishment. Our awareness of the detrimental consequences of being a slave to a cigarette, alcohol or drugs, is capable of activating our logic and willpower and hence of taking us out of a dependency on intoxicants.

Intoxicants are a source of short-term pleasure. Our affinity with using them, often masks some serious weaknesses in a person. The pleasure-field of this kind can turn into a heavy battlefield, which will provide an opportunity for the person to terminate their slavery to those hazardous substances. If the person manages to revive their logic and to generate sufficient willpower, they are likely to transcend the weaknesses related to that trouble. However, the final result of such a battle is inevitably in concord with the destiny plan of the individual.

Our efforts cannot change our destiny. The authority to make such an intervention belongs to the celestial powers that administer the Existential Programmes. They can even influence our thought chains and hence lead us into necessary experiences, in order to make us complete certain evolutionary stages. Have you ever wondered how an occasion made you think, and therefore act in a certain way, which resulted in what appeared to be a disaster? How often, though, have we realised that those unpleasant events later worked to our advantage?

The celestial powers also protect us, even though we are not aware of their workings. Our Guardian Friends have always been busy guiding us through experiences, and supervising our evolvement.

Pleasure and pain

Man must exercise temperance and control of his senses and leanings in every way, thus keeping himself young in body and mind. – Nikola Tesla

We are evolving energies embodied on Earth, in order to clear *karma*[69] and make progress in the evolution of our consciousness. We come here alone and will leave this world alone – taking not a single material possession with us, not even our material body. Our real abode is not the dimensional energy of Earth, and Nikola Tesla, who never owned a dwelling, hinted at this by saying – that he could not possibly settle in a home on Earth, when his real belongings were not of this world.

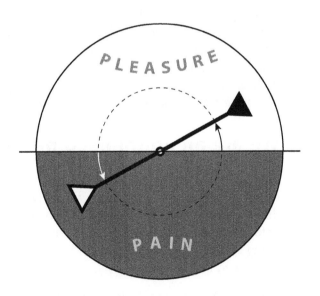

We are like actors, who put on a costume to use during the play on this planet only. When the show is over, we leave the costume for the planet to recycle it. However, one day, we will claim an everlasting costume and take it with us into other realities.

Living within the material realm on Earth is both a pleasurable and painful experience.

Pleasure and pain are faces of the same coin. Here, on Earth, one will inevitably experience both of its sides – due to the nature of the life programme written for this planet. We are certainly not going to object to this programme. In the same way as we cannot influence the life of the characters in a book or a movie but accept their destinies, we are to accept our personal destiny too. Translated into the level of everyday affairs, this attitude would spare us from many unnecessary ups and downs since we accept everything that comes our way – both people and events. This behaviour will enhance our inner peace and social harmony.

Humans are capable of noticing the pleasure/pain mechanism, and of achieving maturity pertaining to material things and money. Parallel to their evolvement in this field, tests and exams will decrease and eventually come to an end.

Sex is not to be confused with love

The primal function of sexual activity is to secure the continuation of the race, which is regulated as an instinctive impulse. However, in addition, sexual activity also needs to be experienced to the point of saturation, so that an individual can attain a spiritual culture.

Sexual pursuit is not to be confused with love. In a sex-driven relationship, desire stays on the carnal level – but an individual is bigger than the physical body alone. Thus, after saturation point with sex, we evolve to eventually experience love from within our own essence, relating exclusively to the essences of others. At that stage, we consciously love all beings, and in an equal manner. We recognise others and relate to them beyond the level of our physical desires.

We are an epitomised natural power

This beautiful planet is a medium that has been carefully designed to provide evolutionary tests for all those who dwell on it. Tests start in our thought dimension and are completed through our behaviour. Tests are not presented before we are capable of passing them, though sometimes numerous attempts, along several lifetimes, are needed to make us adopt a new approach in order to succeed in a single test.

Here, on Earth, people live largely unaware of the power of their genetic potential, bestowed on them by the Creator, and still experience themselves in the medium of a predominantly dualistic consciousness. Continuous challenges come our way, and our weak points keep popping up. However, no matter how fragile and imperfect we might appear to ourselves, we are an epitomised natural power capable of succeeding in all exams.

CONDITIONINGS AND TABOOS

Conditioning

Taboos and conditionings hold us back by preventing the expansion of our awareness. However, the conditionings and taboos should not be blamed for that situation, but rather the people who have sealed their own awareness. Such people prefer the shelter of familiar energies rather than excursions beyond them.

To a conditioned mind, old patterns are the best patterns, and an established scale of values is good enough to last forever. Such a mind has no need to question; it has no need for experiencing new and different ways either.

The behaviour of conditioned persons is therefore rather predictable. Their automatic responses and mental rigidity make them more like robots than human beings – because humans, by the nature of their design, continuously aspire to get better and do so by mentally transcending energies. Open-mindedness is crucial for this ascension.

Since new energy/information hardly penetrates a conditioned mind, truth, which is subject to time-energy, is beyond their reach. The entire evolvement of a conditioned person is therefore slow or even temporarily suspended. Such people can never know themselves, and can be hostages of their own restricted awareness for a long time.

Life is a perfect programme, broad enough to include solutions for even such cases as sealed awareness. So, sooner or later, a conditioned mind will get into situations that will require the breaking of the shell around the conditioning. Under the constant and increasing pressure of time-energy, those stiff mental shells will have an opportunity to loosen, and so allow the expansion of awareness. In other words, cosmic currents stimulate awareness and growth of consciousness of people purified enough to receive these off-planetary influences. To others, the same currents are useless for as long as they cannot attract and process them. Consequently, such individuals fail to evolve parallel to the demand of the energy present on the planet during their lifetime.

Taboos

Taboos are a form of conditioned thinking, based on moral judgment and religious belief. Taboos request particular abstinences, and are present widely in social groups.

To a conditioned mind, breaking a taboo is an unthinkable option, and even changing an opinion on any matter is seen as a weakness. It is difficult to believe that a conditioned mind is concerned with the notion of progress at all.

Conditioned, conservative and taboo-inclined individuals cannot reach certain dimensions with their thought frequencies. So, they fail to attract the currents that will make them happy.

Evolvement is the elevation of our frequencies, registered in our essence.

JEALOUSY

Jealousy is the inability to perceive somebody else's success in a positive way. A jealous person can even exert effort that will belittle more fortunate people, or work against them in such a way as to inflict damage on their position.

Extreme jealousy is harmful to our health because it overemphasises differences and the individualistic stance – all of which are contrary to the vital existential principles, such as *mutual support* and *integration*. This kind of jealousy attracts low vibrational energy into our body.

However, jealousy can be used as a motivating factor to prompt a person to work on themselves, in order to reach what others already have and what they are jealous about – be it stronger muscles, the latest model of a car, or more friends.

NEGATIVITIES

The low frequencies that we operate through separate us from the divine light of our essence. Our negative attitudes and behaviour contribute to maintaining that distance. Nevertheless, dwelling in negative thoughts is simply our deeply rooted habit.

To speed up our evolvement through these final stages of human evolution, all *negative thoughts*[70] generated on our planet are currently made to return to their senders. This mechanism, provided by the technological intervention of the celestial authorities, is in the form of a magnetic screen placed around the Earth's atmosphere to filter the thought energy emanating from our world. Thoughts issued with a good intention pass through that magnetic sieve, and continue towards the fulfilment of their cosmic purpose and destiny.

Negative thoughts, bounced back to their initial location, will affect the person who has produced them. Hence, such individuals fall into the pit that they themselves have dug by thinking negatively.

Negative thoughts carry negative electricity, which is also released by the brain waves of people who suffer from depression. Unless we clear our minds of all negative thoughts, we will remain imprisoned by our own selves. As a consequence, our fits of depression will continue to exhaust us. What could take us out of this cycle are our innate mechanisms such as common sense, conscience and willpower.

Liberation from negative thoughts, as well as from other conditionings, is the field of greatest struggle an individual has to face. All other battles are much easier, however difficult they might seem to be. Each liberation from an obsolete thought pattern releases lots of energy, which was locked up – by the power of belief, or by an inert mind. The released energy thence becomes available to be used in a new way.

Every person on our planet is responsible for creating his own heaven and hell.

Positive thoughts and attitudes make us see goodness and beauty around us, and they open us to more pleasant experiences. On the other hand, negative thoughts cause an energy imbalance in our physical constitution, which leads to a faster deterioration of our health.

Even though our essence is positive, its emanations depend on our thoughts. When we complete the evolution of our essence, it will be able to filter negative thoughts. Thence, we will spread only positive vibrations.

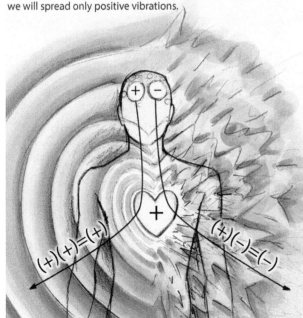

When faced with the unpleasant situation of being accused by somebody, the best response would be to send love to the person instead of criticism, and to refrain from being defensive. Then, we could focus on meeting at the common coordinates. This behaviour will demonstrate that we have transcended the need to prove our point by clinging to a dualistic view.

cosmic energy is negative

water evaporates
and forms clouds;
clouds and rain
are negative

positive-thinking people
attract cosmic energy

plants and animals are positive[143]

PASSIONS

Passion is a strong longing for particular experiences. It can be focused on almost anything in life – even on counting the number of trains that pass a certain spot. The usual passions are to do with collecting specific items or achieving a professional goal. There are also people passionate in their search for knowledge and truth.

Passion is based on desire. What makes the distinction between passion and desire is the degree of enthusiasm involved. It is only overwhelmingly strong desire that turns into passion. Interestingly, genuine enthusiasm is generated from troubles, rather than from a comfortable life, and is a precious evolutionary achievement.

Every passion is a potential black hole

Passions can take over our willpower and enslave us. They can even blind our mind, and pull us into regrettable experiences. Every passion is therefore a potential black hole that can deplete our energy and time, and lock us into a particular stage of evolvement. For that reason, it is crucial to tame our tendencies for passions. They are dangerous because they can hinder our evolution.

If our self-awareness, logic and willpower are inadequate, passions can easily bypass our control and govern our actions. Passion for eating chocolate, or watching *Formula 1* races, can therefore lead to an addiction to the feelings behind those experiences.

Addiction and *obsession*[71] are close siblings. In both cases the person in question lacks the strength to move on to the behaviour of a higher energy plane.

Passions hold us in a terrestrial consciousness

Pleasures derived from excessive passions debilitate rather than empower a person. With the passing of time, it then becomes more difficult to face the real origin of passions, and to achieve liberation from their grip.

Passions hold us in a terrestrial consciousness. Since evolvement is a continuous process of accommodating to higher energies, being a slave to passions indicates our incapacity to transcend particular energy thresholds. It is as if a person stops evolving some aspects of their personality, letting their logic and willpower hibernate.

It is not harmful to have passions, if we do not become their slaves.

EGO

loving person   ego driven person

Two sides of ego

Ego is the sense of the *self*, of *me*, of who I am. Ego has a very powerful potential and has been introduced to facilitate the survival of humans as well as to ensure their terrestrial progress. However, our ego is a precious asset only when it acts constructively or is consumed by a positive service, otherwise it can become one's greatest enemy. Who uses their ego constructively? – Primarily, artists do. If they were not equipped with a sufficient sense of ego, the world would hardly ever hear about the artwork of even geniuses. Ego prompts artists to disseminate their work.

Ego is useful in building a sense of individuality – though, only if it does not overtake the entire persona of the individual. If it does, our ego will pull us back and thus hinder our evolution.

Since it resists the accepting of change and so our moving forward, our ego obstructs the flow of energy. Ego also never gives without expecting something in return because in its consideration the self has the prime interest. It is due to prevailing egotistical behaviour, which impacts on the quality of energy in our environment, that difficult life conditions are being created – both for the individual and on the planetary level. Unfortunately, it seems that people still fail to assess the proportion of damage that an uncontrolled ego can inflict.

In the view of ego, our personal goals have priority. However, too strong an intensity of that focus can upset the balance created by our conscience, in which case we shamelessly ignore others and the planet.

Ego is incapable of holding a bigger picture, as if *me* is the centre of the entire creation, and the most valuable entity to invest in – for nothing else can match its importance. This attitude makes it impossible for such a person to fully integrate with society.

Our ego also obstructs our path to wisdom, because it prevents us from asking questions by assuming it knows all the answers already.

Can ego let us integrate?

Our ego sees no alternative to itself, so is extremely difficult to tame. As it is self-serving, the ego is even able to upset established orders and compromise social wellbeing. If we still wonder why the sacred texts hinted that Adam and Eve were disqualified from entering Heaven, perhaps ego could be the one of the culprits searched for over the centuries. It is interesting to ponder if ego would ever accept this proposal.

To reach the *Heaven* the sacred books were talking about, an individual would need to evolve to the level of that dimension and thus deserve it. Therefore, when the requisite personality and physical qualities are attained, the entrance to the Dimension of Heaven is permitted. In this context, *Hell* would denote *living without attaining the necessary development*, due to one's incapacity to progress through the range of energies compulsory for reaching Heaven. Such people are destined to live in the discomfort of their own imperfections, amplified by the imperfections of others who are at the same level – below the threshold of Heaven.

The evolvement, ascension, and integration processes, are obstructed by our ego, and we will hardly be successful in gaining them if we do not break our ego-chains. Thus the biggest enemy to our dreams, about a happy world with a lasting peace, are us – in other words, our ego, which by its definition separates us from others in order to give us a sense of individual identity. Until we solve this inner, personal, contradiction – we will live in a troubled world of harsh reality unable to reach an inner peace and harmony. When we attain sufficient self-awareness, self-criticism, conscience and willpower, we will be able to manifest a world of happy people.

To obliterate ego, a person needs to transcend their own self-importance. Those who manage to do that, reach their essence-consciousness, and so are considered godlike.

5 INNER MECHANISMS

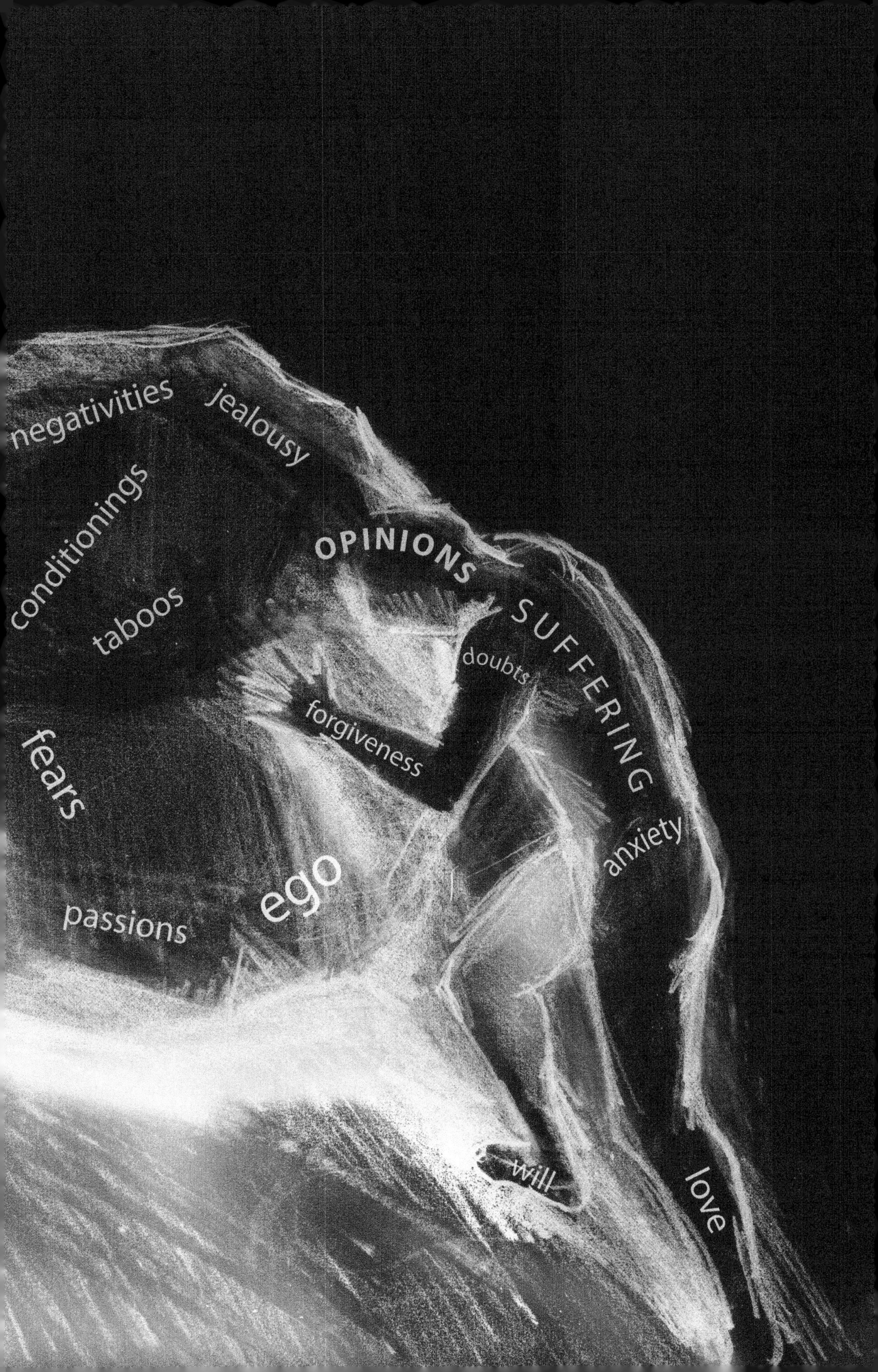

negativities
jealousy
conditionings
OPINIONS
taboos
SUFFERING
doubts
forgiveness
fears
anxiety
ego
passions
will
love

DOUBTS AND QUEST

Doubts

Doubts are a useful mechanism which leads us towards universal consciousness. They are meant to prompt our search for the answers and truths acceptable to us.

Only a powerful awareness can doubt since it is not inclined to believe in everything. This is a protective role of doubt. If following our doubts we undertake necessary exploration and acquire knowledge – that is how doubts serve our evolution and lead us towards light.

Doubts spring from the activity of the left side of the brain, fired by cerebral logic. The more dominant in our mental activity that side of the brain is, the more space for doubts there will be.

The presence of too many doubts may also indicate that a person has not been purified enough to develop self-confidence and a significant spiritual culture. Doubting individuals are often hesitant in drawing conclusions and making choices as if they lack the capacity to fully trust both themselves and life.

One can continue doubting all one's life, which will surely happen for as long as such a person does not develop sufficient faith.

Faith combats doubts by introducing a bigger picture that includes metaphysical realm. It opens a space for accepting things, which are not entirely explicable or known. The faculty of faith is hosted by the right brain hemisphere. To become a balanced person, our brain hemispheres surely need to be harmonised; rationality and intuition need to find common ground.

Those who lack faith can struggle to reach their inner peace and happiness. They might burn in the cauldron of doubts over essential existential questions – that our mind will have difficulty answering, unless it merges with our essence.

The human mind needs to understand and accept that an individual is bigger than their mind. Therefore, it is not our mind alone that is entitled to inform us on existential truths. There is also human essence, with its own logic and consciousness, which our mind needs to recognise and learn to collaborate with. Doubts open the pathways between the logic of our mind and logic of our essence.

If we are doubtful, but passive, we can become negative. If doubts are treated constructively, through a quest, they can lead us to new energies and clarity.

For as long as people have doubts, they will look for miracles. However, those who possess true faith need no miracles – they trust their own understanding and knowledge. This is not to say that people of faith are devoid of logic.

The path of doubts is a necessary evolutionary phase, which leads us towards the light and universal truth.

Quest

Quest takes us on a road of self-discovery and so we start searching for information that is meaningful and supportive to our personal energy field. Guidance is rather instinctive and operates as curiosity. Signposts mark myriads of directions, hence is ever so easy to get lost.

Too much curiosity, or too much information, can distract us. To find a balance, is a constant challenge because there are also contradicting tendencies in our own selves. Throughout a quest various inner alignments take place, as well as the discovery of new ways of fitting into society and life itself.

A quest advances through forming and posing questions to our own selves, not to others, and by finding the answers through personal experiences.

When we search genuinely and perseveringly enough, we eventually find what we have really been looking for – the self. The only thing left undone then is to transcend the self and reach the essence-self.

If our curiosity is exhausted, it means we have accomplished our quest. Thereafter we know that when we do not get everything we wished for, it is because we already have what we need. We comprehend that our most precious property is already within us. It is the essence-potential of the godly substance, inseparable asset of each godly seed.

By calming our mind and following our conscience, we can tap into the communication plane in which essences talk to one another. That communication medium is made up of the vibrations that feed our essence-gene. Hence an active conscience accelerates our evolution.

The Power we have been dreaming about, is dreaming about us too. It is the single dream present in the entire creation: the dream of a particle about the whole it originates from, the dream of our omnipotent essence-seed about its returning home. Infinite voids and infinite frequencies are held together by the intangible streams of those longings.

FORGIVENESS

A person eager to change and move on, can easily forgive.

Holding negative emotions against somebody is an unhealthy load to carry around. It obstructs some of our inner energy pathways, and potentially leads to more clogging. The bigger an unresolved issue is, the bigger is the obstacle to our inner peace, good health and happiness. Clearing those emotional black holes is done through forgiveness.

By acting in a manner of forgiveness, we accept that we do not need to win in every situation in life. We also accept that neither we nor the other party is perfect, and despite all of that – everything is fine and life is a beautiful opportunity to learn about ourselves. Every time we forgive, we are elevated closer to a better self.

It is very difficult to practice self-forgiveness. As a matter of fact, the only forgiving we need to make happen is that one, because it is not others who have lead us to a particular hurting experience, but we ourselves. Hence we need to forgive ourselves for behaving as we did, and for choosing to be hurt. Such an attitude implies taking full responsibility for our own behaviour and its consequences.

As we perform self-forgiving, we truly accept who we are – even though we are aware of our imperfections and their repercussions. Forgiving ourselves is an act of unconditional love.

If we manage to conduct our behaviour properly, we would be unlikely to experience unpleasant situations. Also, we are the sole captain of our ship therefore we have no right to blame anybody else for what transpires on our ship, or for the direction in which it is heading.

The captain in us is also responsible for our emotions, and so has to exercise effective supervision over them. To avoid feeling hurt, an unconditional acceptance of every situation is necessary. If we were to choose to feel grateful for each experience, regardless of the behaviour of others, we would come from a truly noble position. So, however unpleasantly or unfairly others behave towards us, it is not just about forgiving them. It is primarily about accepting them as they are and accepting us as we are.

Apologising, and asking for forgiveness from those we have upset or mistreated, would be a gesture of humility, performed by our mature persona that accepts its own insignificance in the vastness of creation. Such an individual prostrates himself before the orders and the laws of the universe, and appreciates equally a human being, an animal and a blade of grass.

On the topic of forgiveness, in order to facilitate the process of purification and evolvement, the sacred books suggest a frequent self-assessment of our thoughts and behaviour. Upon such a pondering, a confession of wrongdoings needs to be performed. The sacred buildings, which have been acting as God's consulates on Earth, have even designated places for this ritual.

Asking forgiveness from God is a profound inner exercise that potentially re-establishes disturbed orders – like opening a new programme from a higher coordinates of awareness. This exercise has not lost its validity, regardless of the name we give to the Ultimate Power from whom we ask forgiveness for our misbehaviour.

SUFFERINGS AND ANXIETY

Suffering

In the sacred books much has been written about suffering yet the question is whether the role of suffering, pertaining to the evolution of human being, has been understood properly. Contrary to popular view, the function of suffering is highly beneficial because suffering purifies and strengthens us.

In the circumstances of significant life-comfort, the evolvement of humans is usually insufficient because they readily neglect common sense and logic, and are inclined to slip into over-indulgence in various pleasures. An individual can therefore enslave their own self, faster than any outside power could do, and

so remain at the same evolvement juncture for far too long. Hence if the evolvement of an individual does not follow their personal evolutionary trajectory forecasted in the celestial charts, a programme of suffering is inevitably activated. Suffering stimulates the spiritual growth of the person and balances things out – in line with the cause-effect law and the *law of natural equilibrium*[72].

In the programme of suffering, sorrow and regret are the keys to unlock spiritual vibrations. These vibrations are positive energies that purify us from unhealthy thoughts and feelings. If we fail to learn our evolutionary lessons while living in comfort, and if we do not find the right measure for all our pleasures, we will most likely learn necessary lessons through suffering. For evolvement is our inherent and unavoidable path, and is subject to an automatic application of the Existential Programmes. Thus, humans will both suffer and thrive as the universal laws command.

Only a person who is deeply rooted in terrestrial consciousness experiences suffering by considering it as an injustice. Universal consciousness observes life on Earth from a bigger picture. For that reason, it attributes a different meaning to each pain or distress and hence more easily goes through all the challenges.

spiritual vibrations

Universal consciousness uses universal, not terrestrial, logic and reasoning. People who are at this level of evolvement also understand that there are valid causes behind even unpleasant experiences. Hence, even in the hardest of situations they do not complain, or feel unfortunate or mistreated by life.

However paradoxical it might sound, bitter experience and anguish strengthen both our spiritual and physical cellular potential. For that reason, we better appreciate them as our opportunity to evolve, and see them as gifts from life rather than fear them in distress. By understanding and accepting the purpose of suffering, we can gradually become less affected by it – and eventually grow out of that particular programme.

Some consider the phenomenon of suffering to be the greatest argument that God does not exist. According to their view point, God cannot possibly exist and be so merciless by allowing suffering to take place. They would also reason: if God is an Ultimate Power, how come He is unable to stop the painful experiences of people. Yet, what do we truly know about the programme of life on this planet, in other solar systems, galaxies, universes or even in the dimensions beyond them? We, human beings on Earth, have not even scientifically explained the origin of natural energy or the occurrence of some tangibles such as plants or animals – quite apart from spiritual phenomena. Our preconceptions and arrogant blindness are harmful, and have always been working against us – if only our ego would let us notice it!

Peculiarly, both unpleasant and pleasant situations are experienced for the same reason, and that is to facilitate our evolution in the most efficient way.

Anxiety

Anxiety[73] is the state of being in which we, purely subjectively, perceive a situation as threatening or potentially dreadful. These anticipations are often over something unlikely to happen, and are not to be confused with fear – which is a response to a genuine danger.

Anxiety can displace us from our comfortable coordinates and can shake us quite profoundly. In order to restore our inner balance, we need to generate energy. Hence, a fresh perception and approach are helpful.

With a new light, reached by our mental efforts in transcending the distress caused by anxiety, a shift in awareness happens. Each anxiety shock directs us deeper towards our inner self, where we gradually build a focal point of stability and true power.

To those who are purely in the terrestrial consciousness, the doors of the divine light of the universe are closed. The frequency of anxiety has the potential to connect us to that light, which then stimulates our brain synapses and brings new clarity to our thinking. Even though anxiety is an unpleasant state, if it is not pathological, it helps us advance towards a lasting happiness – since it combats our mental inertia and prompts us towards the most solid enthusiasm.

The road to happiness is multifaceted and requires an integration of all aspects of our persona. In that process, the evolution of our thought, our consciousness and our cellular potential are paramount. As we evolve, our capacity to think, to acquire knowledge, and to attain consciousness, while learning the universal truths, steadily grows. However, terrestrial academic knowledge as well as any material wealth are not enough to open the door of true happiness for us. The keys of that door are anxiety and suffering; hence the importance of unpleasant experiences. They are our opportunities to ponder deep inside ourselves and make valuable spiritual experiences out of them.

Spiritual experiences purify us so that we can receive more spiritual energy. That energy is not from our world but from the spiritual plane of advanced universal dimensions. It is the energy of our essence-self. We attract spiritual energy by means of our brain, from where this energy is distributed to our cells. The more spiritual energy we receive to our spiritually-hungry bodily vessel, the faster we approach the perfect state of a human, marked by spiritual fulfilment.

Eternal happiness is offered to a highly evolved individual only. Peculiarly, anxiety plays important role in that process.

RESURRECTION

After a millennia of functioning through terrestrial consciousness here on Earth, humans have reached a significant evolutionary threshold. They are now transiting into the next consciousness *modus operandi*, known as *cosmic consciousness* (leading to *infinite awareness* and *infinite consciousness*). This evolutionary stage has been announced in religious books through the notion of *resurrection*[74].

Beside our consciousness, what also resurrect are our thoughts and our essence. Thought gradually gets its proper form – since to know how to think is the result of a long evolution. Unless we gain supremacy over our thoughts, we cannot claim our personal energy-treasures from the universal archives. The true sovereign of a future *happy*

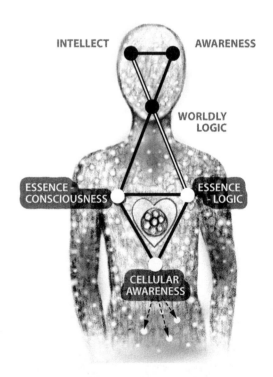

INTELLECT   AWARENESS

WORLDLY LOGIC

ESSENCE - CONSCIOUSNESS   ESSENCE - LOGIC

CELLULAR AWARENESS

world[75] is going to be correct human thought.

With terrestrial attitudes only, we cannot make the required evolutionary progress. Hence the programme of *learning through experience* makes us broaden our terrestrial outlook. This necessary widening of our observational field comes sooner or later, and we attain a universal view on what is going on with us and around us.

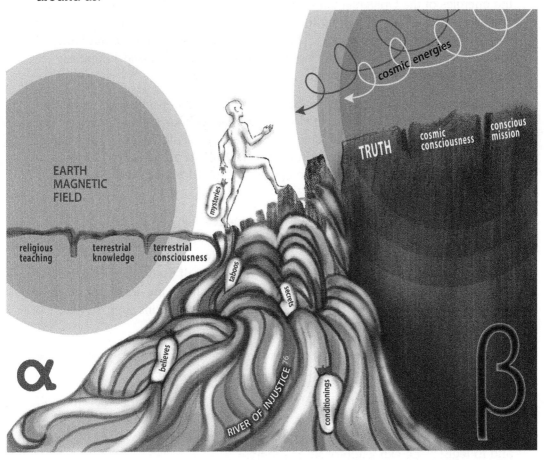

Our experiences, also, steadily melt away the layers between our persona and our essence. Consequently, our essence-values start to dominate our behaviour. The way our logic operates changes as well, shifting from the patterns of terrestrial logic to the patterns of universal (essence) logic. Our consciousness therefore gradually expands and transcends the dimension it operates in.

Resurrection also means waking up to the universal laws and truth. However, universal information and knowledge cannot be reached unless we complete our training through the religious doctrines, and do away with religious conditionings. For, religious education is the first stage the Divine Plan has applied on us, as preparation for our evolvement through the energies of the Universal dimension.

CHANGING WITH THE ENERGY OF TIME

All knowledge acquired on Earth so far is just a springboard for evolution through the energies of the Universal dimension – which are brand new energies for our entire civilisation. Accumulating those unknown energies inside our cells is our current evolutionary imperative. They will prepare us for the life-mediums of our future habitats, in the dimensions of eternal tranquillity and happiness we currently cannot even conceive of.

The permission for moving to higher evolutionary dimensions is gained after some necessary preparation in the lower dimensions. Our physical constitution, our thought patterns and our entire personality need to change, and adjust beforehand to the quality common to the next higher dimension. Our energy composition is therefore subjected to upgrading, in order to suit our evolutionary journey.

This process is facilitated by the cosmic influences sent from the *open sky*[77], according to the cosmic destiny of Earth and life on it. Our capacity to respond to these influences is crucial for our growth and even our survival. Changing parallel to time-energy means that we can make use of that energy. Hence our awareness unveils and, fed with energy particles from the incoming cosmic currents, we ultimately figure out the answers to the questions such as *Who we are* and *Why we are here on Earth, and why now*.

In each period, energy sent to the planet matches the evolutionary needs of the entire creation on it.

Those able to receive cosmic energy, benefit from the time they live in, and surely evolve faster. Thus, gradually, time-energy modifies a human, as well as all life-forms on Earth. No wonder, biologists continue to discover new species and to register the extinction of some others.

THE PURPOSE OF LIFE

Our life on Earth has an evolutionary objective. That objective is to discover the truth of our ultimate purpose, and to manifest it, in the light of an awareness which transcends our planet. In other words, we come to discern our meaning on the canvas of life, and to live it.

As a matter of fact, whether aware of it or not, each energy which is brought into existence, including the one operating as a human being, does nothing but perform its purpose according to the orders of the universe, as defined by the unchanging universal laws. However, undertaking that mission consciously is a triumph of the evolving energy in question. Humans on our planet are at the threshold of that crowning stage.

Our evolution is a path involving the enhancing of our ability to host increasingly higher energies within our cellular and mental structures. Those energies are primarily attracted by our brain, in proportion to its power. However, mental pathways within the brain are opened and fortified according to the evolutionary level of our thought.

The human brain and thought are part of a cosmic energy circuit. The cosmic *Mechanism of Influence*[78] takes us within its domain by the first question a child asks. From then on, the thought of that individual begins to mature.

Energy delivered into our brain generator by our thoughts is the life-potential on which the entire body functions. Hence, the more our brain works, the more our cellular structure will be strengthened – both the physical aspect of the cells and their awareness.

HUMAN EVOLUTION ON EARTH[79]

Ω exit

α entrance

Should the cosmic source, from which our thoughts originally come, close – the human body will cease to live.

We are biological robots actuated and oriented through the power we call *thought*. As our life-potential grows, different facets of awareness within our brain compartments are gradually activated. That process prepares the ground for the expansion of our consciousness. All those changes reflect on our personality and so we transform.

As a part of the cosmic energy network, even though we live on Earth, our meaning is of a cosmic origin and significance.

85

Layers of knowledge

According to the universal ordinances, solar systems are classified into *Solar dimensions*[80] – depending on the frequencies and the intensity of energies found in them. Hence, each solar dimension has its specific evolutionary dimension (pertaining to its frequencies) and an energy dimension (pertaining to the intensity of its energy). Though separated when it comes to their classification, in actuality these dimensional frequency/energy layers are an integrated whole.

To enter the next higher evolutionary dimension, we first need to be able to assimilate energies of the dimensions well above it. For example, in order to enter the 4th Evolutionary dimension from the 3rd Evolutionary dimension, it is necessary to receive the energy of the 9th Evolutionary dimension. The sacred book, the *New Testament*, was prepared in that very dimension, and sent to our planet through the programme of Jesus Christ. This Holy Prophet emanated frequencies of love and, similarly, the sacred book he dictated converged on the frequency of divine love. With the *New Testament*, humanity was offered the evolutionary path through the *7 layers of terrestrial knowledge*[81].

As a part of the same order of evolution, known as the *Third Order of the Lord*, the programme of the prophet Mohammed opened six centuries later and a new sacred book, *Koran*, was conveyed to introduce further dimensional energies to Earth (the energies up to the 18th Evolutionary dimension).

However, in *Koran*, only the information given through the energy of up to the 9th Evolutionary dimension was presented overtly. Hence *Koran*, which brought specific knowledge on social order, also facilitates the evolution necessary for reaching the 4th Evolutionary dimension, called *Heaven*. Information that carries the energy from beyond the 9th Evolutionary dimension (10th – 18th), has been ciphered in order to protect humans of that time from dimensional energies too strong for them. Over the centuries, only a certain number of individuals has managed to unlock the energy of the hidden advanced dimensions, and they derived deeper understanding and knowledge from this sacred book. *Koran* carries the *7 layers of the celestial knowledge*[82].

The 5th Evolutionary dimension is called *Karena*[83]. During the usual evolutionary progress, we leave our crude-matter body behind – and enter *Karena* by our light-body only.

Karena has seven "stations". In the first two stations (2 *tranquil times*), our light-body is reinforced by incombustible energies and engrafted by the energies of the three planets of our solar system that precede the *asteroid zone*[84]. Then, through the five stations of *supreme times* the preparation of a foetus, which will live as a human beyond the 5th Evolutionary dimension, takes place. The cells of that foetus are engrafted by the energy of the remaining five planets within our solar system that are beyond the asteroid zone.

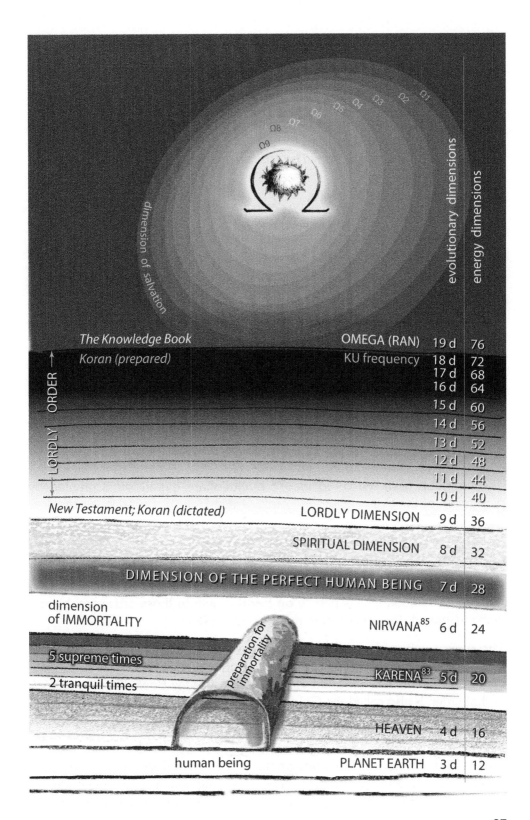

The Knowledge Book	OMEGA (RAN)	19 d	76
Koran (prepared)	KU frequency	18 d	72
		17 d	68
		16 d	64
		15 d	60
		14 d	56
		13 d	52
		12 d	48
		11 d	44
		10 d	40
New Testament; Koran (dictated)	LORDLY DIMENSION	9 d	36
	SPIRITUAL DIMENSION	8 d	32
	DIMENSION OF THE PERFECT HUMAN BEING	7 d	28
dimension of IMMORTALITY	NIRVANA[85]	6 d	24
5 supreme times			
2 tranquil times	KARENA[83]	5 d	20
	HEAVEN	4 d	16
human being	PLANET EARTH	3 d	12

dimension of salvation

evolutionary dimensions

energy dimensions

ORDER

LORDLY

preparation for immortality

Ω9 Ω8 Ω7 Ω6 Ω5 Ω4 Ω3 Ω2 Ω1

Karena prepares an immortal biological human body. Only such a body is able to endure the energy intensity and the frequency that start from the 6th Evolutionary dimension (also called the *Dimension of Immortality* or *Nirvana*[85]).

The final 7 knowledge layers on our way to the dimension of a fully genetically realised human, considered a *perfect human*, are of the *universal knowledge*. This knowledge is already available on Earth. It has come from the 19th Evolutionary dimension, called *Omega*, with *The Knowledge Book*[86] dictated in the period 1981-1993.

The Knowledge Book is bestowed on Earth from beyond the Religious dimension, and offers a curriculum based on the universal energies communicated to our planet for the first time in the form of a book. Its frequency conveys explicit universal laws and truth.

Owing to specific reasons for an *accelerated evolution*[144] during the 20th, 21st and 22nd centuries, *The Knowledge Book*, with the *light-photon-cyclone technique*[87] inherent in it, has been prepared to help us evolve through the 7th Evolutionary dimension in this lifetime. Hence, the book offers an evolutionary shortcut (bypassing our light body's going to *Karena*).

The *Far East Philosophies* provide the evolutionary path towards the 6th Evolutionary dimension – through individual efforts in rigorous spiritual purification that includes the use of great solitude. However, to move on to the level of human perfection, individual evolutionary endeavours primarily focused on the self are not sufficient.

The transition from the 6th to the 7th Evolutionary dimension is granted by permission of the *System*[88] of the Lordly Order. Hence, a conscious service to humanity suggested by this System enables success in evolvement through the 7th Evolutionary dimension.

The Knowledge Book introduces the System and explains its own role and the function of the System in the context of the unification processes throughout the universe. The book invites people on Earth to join in those processes, by first working towards the uniting of humanity on the planet.

The current universal unification movement is dedicated to building a *Golden Age*[89]. The existential order created for and during the Golden Age is considered the Fourth and final order of the Lord. *The Knowledge Book*, the pivotal book of that order, is also called the *Golden Book of the Golden Age*.

The cosmic technology inherent in *The Knowledge Book* empowers every individual who reads it, and accelerates their evolution beyond what was ever possible in the history of humanity on this planet. How does it work? The light-photon-cyclone technique utilised in *The Knowledge Book* continuously attracts time-energy onto its letter frequencies. This attracted time-energy, together with the Omega energy of the dimension that the book comes from, is reflected onto each reader – but in proportion to their capacity to receive it. In other words, the book changes its energy according to the evolvement level of the person who reads it.

Owing to its ability to attract the cosmic energy that comes to Earth, the aura of this book continuously changes. By responding to the time-energy and to the evolutionary capacity of its reader, *The Knowledge Book* functions as a living entity. Terrestrial science will explain these unusual properties in the future.

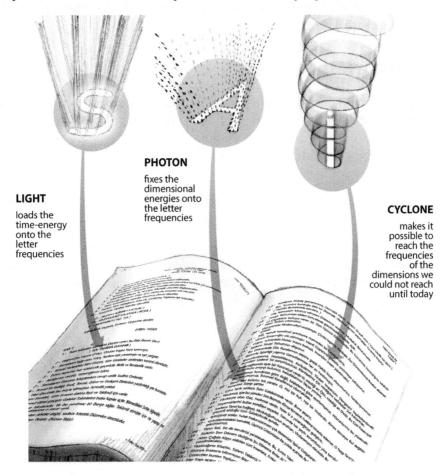

PHOTON

fixes the dimensional energies onto the letter frequencies

LIGHT

loads the time-energy onto the letter frequencies

CYCLONE

makes it possible to reach the frequencies of the dimensions we could not reach until today

With the *The Knowledge Book* on the planet, humanity received incomparable celestial assistance in acquiring of the energy necessary for the realisation of our full genetic potential. If we manifest that potential, as perfect humans, we will have the privilege of existing during the forthcoming Golden Age – in the dimensions of eternal peace and prosperity.

Would humanity recognise how great a favour has been given to this planet by *The Knowledge Book* being sent to it, and make efforts to follow its suggestions?

Also, would human beings take full responsibility for their own evolution and the future of Earth? Yes, they would – should they follow the guidance of their essence and their reasoning triangle: *intellect-logic-awareness*[90].

Regarding our evolvement chart, achieving immortality in itself (*Nirvana*, the 6th Evolutionary dimension) is not the sole aim of our evolution since there are evolvement levels beyond that one. The aim is immortal human beings whose perfection comes from their essence-personality in action; who self-sacrificingly serve humanity while they respect and follow the universal laws. Those are the people of the 7th Evolutionary dimension, the Dimension of Perfection – as *The Knowledge Book* explains.

Reincarnation

The amount of energy we need to assimilate in order to become perfect humans, starting from our earliest existence, is huge – both in quantity and intensity. Since this is too big a task for one lifetime, the programme of reincarnation provides enough opportunities for a gradual evolvement through the necessary energy range.

In the chain of incarnations, we enter into a physical body and then leave it – ideally, each lifetime assimilating more evolutionary energy.

The power of this evolutionary energy is immense; it has the ability to alter crude matter, as well as our spiritual constitution, without being detrimental to our cellular structure. Hence we evolve both as a physical vehicle and as a consciousness.

The energy, which a human being epitomises, is of an outstanding capacity. We are able to continuously transcend our own consciousness, and so to reach the properties of godly essence within us.

From micro- to macro-consciousness

A particle of energy (micro-consciousness) is programmed to reach a macro-consciousness over a long process of transformation. Somewhere on that trajectory, the evolving energy inhabits the physical form of a human.

Energy evolving within a human body is trained to understand itself – first as an individual entity and then as an integral part of the Total. In other words, we are a grain of dust of the living whole but we possess a speck of the essence-energy of the Total. That energy is the source of all our power, and the pathway for our returning to the Total (macro-consciousness).

In the dimensions of form, arranged according to *existential ordinances*[91], humans gradually learn to behave in harmony with those ordinances and eventually choose to comply with them in a conscious way. Such is our *genetic programme*[92] – it makes us surrender to the power and wisdom of the Total that has created us. When a particle reaches the level of the macro-consciousness, it unerringly follows the *Will of the Total*[93] and therefore selflessly manifests that *Will* on its own coordinates.

Surrendering to the Will of the Total

The *will* of humans on Earth is often considered to be *free will* though many would argue against that being the case. On the other hand, the question is whether our *will* can ever have a bigger scope and freedom – bearing in mind both the laws of nature, reflected on the life-medium of this planet, and the limitations originating from our body and from our social norms. Our *will* is expected to comply with all of those. In absolute terms, therefore, our *will* is not free though it operates with a significant amount of freedom.

The *will* of human beings is subject to evolvement. The way a person uses their *will*, depends on the level of consciousness of that person.

Unfortunately, our consciousness and conscience still allow us to primarily think locally instead of globally, and to have aspirations driven by rather individualistic interests. Since we *will* too much for our own selves, our *will* is still not a *Will of the Total*. Our *will* is unevolved therefore incomplete.

For as long as we behave with a narrow awareness by disrespecting society and the needs of the global community, and fail to recognise the sovereignty of the existential ordinances, we will not have the privilege of acting as a conduit for the *Will of the Total*.

How can we reach the *Will of the Total* or when can the *Total Will* be entrusted to us?

There is a *particle* of the *Total Will* inside us. That particle belongs to the universal power and acts as our driving force towards the more advanced dimensions and towards our essence-self. As a representative of the universe inside us, this particle gradually returns us to the wealth of the universal totality.

The particle of the *Total Will* is the base of our *partial will* upon which our *individual will* acts. *Partial will* is the *God-given will*, while *individual will* is the one we give to ourselves by the power of our personality.

As our *individual will* grows stronger, as we claim more essence-energy from the universal totality, we get closer to our essence-being and so to the universe. But only after we have transcended all our fears and conquered our ego, can we surrender to the *Will of the Total*. At that point, *partial, individual* and *Total Will*, become *ONE Will* – one operational circuit.

Even though it might seem as if we would lose a lot by letting go of our *individual will* – it is only an illusion. On the contrary, from the moment our *individual will* starts surrendering to the *Total Will* we become better receivers of the universal energy that is the source of our power.

When we fully accept the *Will of the Total*, we give it priority over our individual wishes. That way we liberate ourselves from the burden of the ego and individualism. Finally then, the universe can have us within the circuit of its mighty energy, which will then effortlessly flow through us.

A significant stage in the evolution of energy, that we epitomise, is marked by reaching the universal coordinates pertaining to our thought, awareness, consciousness and *will*. Before that is accomplished, the *Will of the Total* communicates with us to some extent only – through the faculty known as *common-sense*.

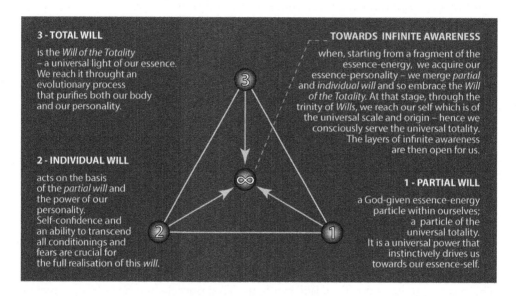

3 - TOTAL WILL

is the *Will of the Totality* – a universal light of our essence. We reach it throught an evolutionary process that purifies both our body and our personality.

2 - INDIVIDUAL WILL

acts on the basis of the *partial will* and the power of our personality. Self-confidence and an ability to transcend all conditionings and fears are crucial for the full realisation of this *will*.

TOWARDS INFINITE AWARENESS

when, starting from a fragment of the essence-energy, we acquire our essence-personality – we merge *partial* and *individual will* and so embrace the *Will of the Totality*. At that stage, through the trinity of *Wills*, we reach our self which is of the universal scale and origin – hence we consciously serve the universal totality. The layers of infinite awareness are then open for us.

1 - PARTIAL WILL

a God-given essence-energy particle within ourselves; a particle of the universal totality. It is a universal power that instinctively drives us towards our essence-self.

SELF-SUPERVISION

A human being's path of self-supervision is often paved with struggle – the struggle with their own self.

Do we, for example, observe our thoughts and our behaviour in every single situation and make responses according to the specifics of those situations or do we, perhaps, still produce automatic responses due to our conditioned mind? Automatic responses would indicate that we are not truly present in the *now*. Instead, we repeat some past behavioural patterns. By doing so, we miss being creative and fail to be refreshed with the cosmic energy of each new moment.

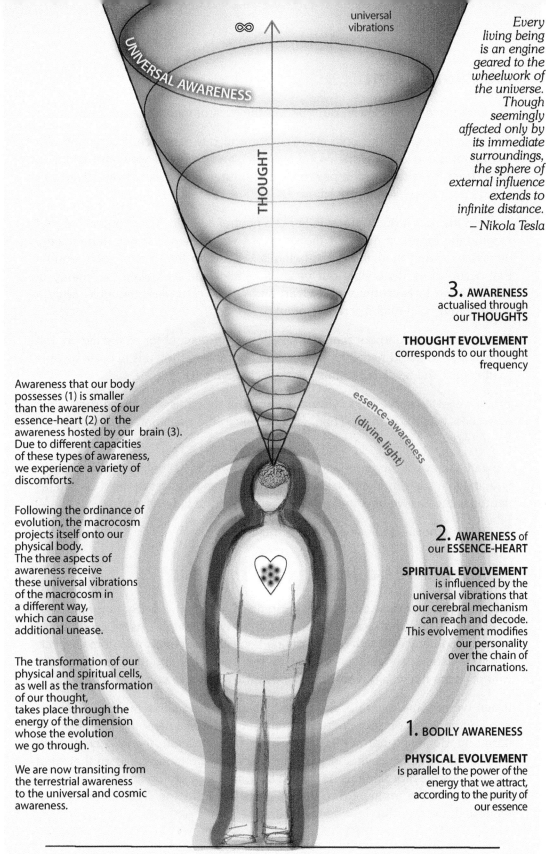

universal vibrations

∞

UNIVERSAL AWARENESS

THOUGHT

Every living being is an engine geared to the wheelwork of the universe. Though seemingly affected only by its immediate surroundings, the sphere of external influence extends to infinite distance.

– Nikola Tesla

3. AWARENESS actualised through our **THOUGHTS**

THOUGHT EVOLVEMENT corresponds to our thought frequency

essence-awareness
(divine light)

Awareness that our body possesses (1) is smaller than the awareness of our essence-heart (2) or the awareness hosted by our brain (3). Due to different capacities of these types of awareness, we experience a variety of discomforts.

Following the ordinance of evolution, the macrocosm projects itself onto our physical body. The three aspects of awareness receive these universal vibrations of the macrocosm in a different way, which can cause additional unease.

The transformation of our physical and spiritual cells, as well as the transformation of our thought, takes place through the energy of the dimension whose the evolution we go through.

We are now transiting from the terrestrial awareness to the universal and cosmic awareness.

2. AWARENESS of our **ESSENCE-HEART**

SPIRITUAL EVOLVEMENT is influenced by the universal vibrations that our cerebral mechanism can reach and decode. This evolvement modifies our personality over the chain of incarnations.

1. BODILY AWARENESS

PHYSICAL EVOLVEMENT is parallel to the power of the energy that we attract, according to the purity of our essence

AS WE PURIFY OURSELVES, VIBRATIONS OF OUR AWARENESS STRETCH INTO FURTHER DISTANCES

Absolute point

The best place to be in, with our mind, is the current moment – the *NOW*.

The *now* moment is the only absolute point in our existence. Everything else outside of it is relative to the *NOW* moment, and pulls our view and attention away from it – either to the past or to the future. Those excursions divert our energy and so weaken our position.

To be in the *now* requires the stability of a neutral attitude. The moment we start judging the faces we meet, or the situations we witness, the *now* time-energy bypasses us, and the lightness of being is lost due to the load of each thought that occupies us. To enable our vessel to attract and assimilate the energy of time, we are to keep the vessel clean and empty of useless thoughts. Only a wakeful mind can fulfil this requirement.

The energy coming to our planet is an evolutionary agent for all the life on it. If we manage to avoid negative, judgemental or fantasy thoughts, we will be able to maximise the receiving of this priceless celestial gift.

When we just observe the environment and our thoughts, an undisturbed, clear awareness acts through us. Then, we are truly in the *now*, and we are one with the life-flow.

We can achieve this control and self-awareness in any situation – in a train, or queuing in a supermarket. By choosing to avoid any useless thought stream, as neutral witnesses we become greater receptors of the time-energy.

To be in the *now* is to be aware and self-aware.

Awareness is a light

The ability to supervise ourselves contributes to making us better human beings in a faster way. What are we to supervise? – Our thoughts, words, emotions, behaviour, interaction with others, eating habits and all other remaining aspects of our personal conduct pertaining to our body and mind. For, numerous sufferings are the result of insufficient power to supervise our own selves.

When we become aware of the impact each of our actions makes on others, and consequently on us, we start to understand the real meaning and effects of harmony. Behaving harmoniously, in any given situation, then becomes both a self-imposed imperative and a pleasure at the same time. We learn that what we hear, see, feel or think, is not worth sharing unless we do so by maintaining the accord of the moment. If our opinion is not fundamentally supportive, or requested, the question is, who needs it?

Human beings start their life with a relatively small domain of awareness. We keep enlarging that domain by encountering new frequencies and by processing them. Even though awareness is hosted by our bodily and spiritual cells, its vibrations expand beyond our body. Hence even without uttering a word, we are eloquent while moving through our environment. People who can get into mutual resonance through the emanations of their awareness, start communicating before they even exchange a single word. Togetherness is born from the instances of these subtle concords.

Awareness bridges the realms of the physical and the metaphysical. The light of it penetrates into the unknown and reveals new meanings to us. Thus, the expansion of our awareness is equally a process of uncovering new meanings.

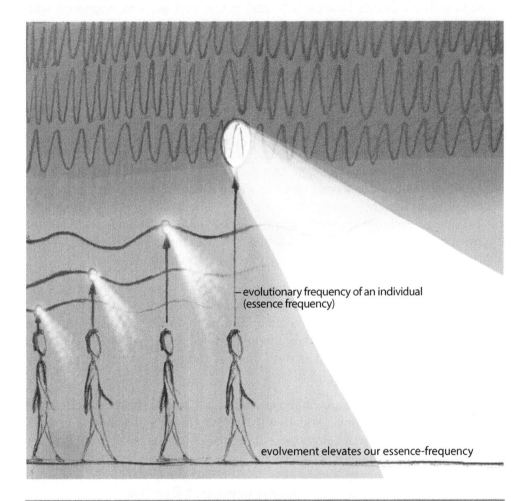

— evolutionary frequency of an individual (essence frequency)

evolvement elevates our essence-frequency

Peace can only come as a natural consequence of Universal enlightenment.
– Nikola Tesla

Silence – order – harmony – beauty

Each of our cells possesses both awareness and consciousness, yet the headquarters of these two faculties is our brain. Though made of flesh and blood, brain is a device like a computer. Its power increases parallel to our evolvement. As we learn to use our brain waves, we also learn to be happy.

The *creation*, which we assume to be *everything-there-is*, started in the *tranquillity of silences* of the unknown primeval void – in which an energy formation programme unfolded through a series of mutations. At the very initial stages of this ancient performance, two dimensions emerged within that void: The Dimension of Tranquillity and the Dimension of Silence. Hence, if we are to align with the planes beyond time and space, and get into resonance with the unified field of primordial powers, a relaxed mind and breath are essential. Alpha brainwave rhythms seem to be instrumental to that activity.

The core cells of the brain, called neurons, produce measurable electrical patterns that are systematised through the frequency ranges. Alpha brainwaves occur at the frequencies of 8 to 12 cycles per second (Hz). They provide harmonisation of the brain hemispheres, and are able to access the knowledge and power of the dimensions beyond what we can reach through other brainwaves.

When our brain, in a wakeful state, operates through the alpha rhythm, we can find solutions to daily challenges and conceive of new scientific and art-related ideas. At that frequency range, the brain's capacity to integrate information is at its highest level. The mental pictures, carried by our brainwaves, seem to be most easily recognised and integrated into the unified fields when flowing through the alpha waves – and so their manifestation is accelerated.

When in the alpha state of mind, with closed eyes, yet wakeful and relaxed, we can project our awareness into the future, into the past, into another person or into ourselves. That way we can acquire information from those time or space destinations, detect other people's thoughts or generate self-healing. Mental effort, or any physical disturbance of this brain rhythm, would immediately affect this capacity.

A silent mind is the property of those who know how to calm their nervous system, and their thoughts, and how to refrain from any intensity in their behaviour. Such a state of being opens up to the powers accessible beyond the turbulence of beta or gamma brain rhythms. In our daily life, in a wakeful state, we operate predominantly through the beta brainwaves (14 – 21 Hz) when our five senses, logic, awareness and consciousness are fully active.

When it comes to the most economical use of our cerebral energy, the order and harmony of our thoughts, as well as our inner peace, are important. These qualities are in the essence of the entire creation and are a concise description

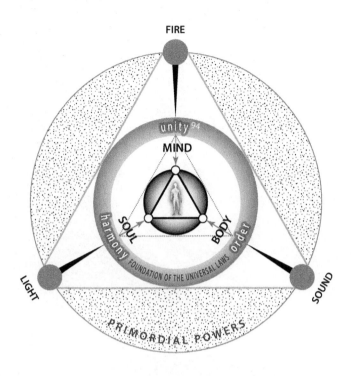

of the BEAUTY of both realms – physical and mental.

The original meaning of the Greek word *cosmos* was *order, beauty* and *harmony*. Pythagoras considered these qualities essential to the world we live in – hence the Greek philosophers used it to refer to the known world.

Later on, alchemists, who considered a human being a small world, extended the meaning of this Greek word into new domains and two new words were coined: *micro-cosmos* (human) and *macro-cosmos* (entire creation). Evidently, long ago, humans were able to recognise the fractal nature of creation as well as the universal significance of beauty.

Beauty is an energy formula, inherent in nature, the manifestation of which nourishes and inspires us. It is an abstract yet perceivable model that the highest forces of creation use to impress themselves elsewhere. While experiencing or creating beauty, we touch our essence.

The capacity to notice, to appreciate and to create order – harmony – beauty is parallel to the level of our consciousness.

Aristotle taught that there was an immovable 'entelechy' in the universe that moves everything and the thought was its main attribute. I am also convinced that the whole universe is unified in both material and spiritual sense. Out there in the universe there is a nucleus that gives us all the power, all the inspiration; it draws us to itself eternally, I feel its mightiness and values it transmits throughout the universe; thus keeping it in harmony. I have not breached the secret of that core, still I am aware of its existence, and when wanting to give it any material attribute I imagine LIGHT, and when trying to conceive it spiritually I imagine BEAUTY and COMPASSION. The one who carries that belief inside feels strong, finds joy in his work, for he experiences himself as a single tone in the universal harmony.
– Nikola Tesla

6 SPROUTING OF OUR ESSENCE

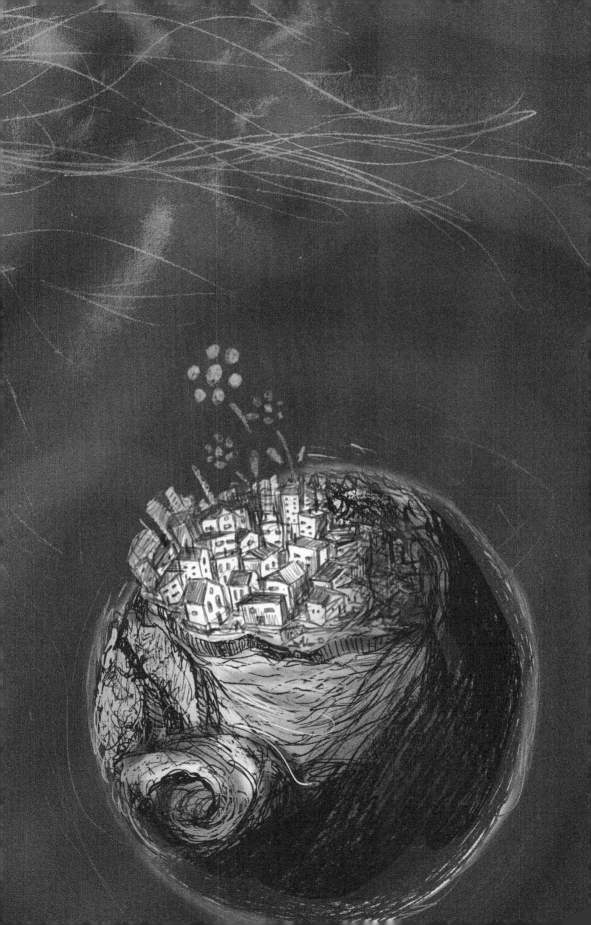

GOODWILL

Goodwill thrives on the enthusiasm of an alert and flexible person, eager to be involved and to give. Such a person does good deeds purely for the sake of it; without the slightest inkling of personal interest. It is the nobility of the ceaseless goodness of their essence, pouring out and prompting them to this kindness.

People of goodwill have transcended the need for their personal comfort zone. They easily respond to the needs of others and without difficulty operate in the magnetic field of those other people. A good-willed person is always ready to be included in both hard work and fun. Tolerant, respectful, supportive, and easygoing, they are precious companions who radiate a lightness of being.

Positivity is inherent in goodwill, hence numerous doors open and solutions get found by this vibrational key. However, if the goodwill is not controlled by intellect and logic, it can be harmful.

CONSCIENCE

Conscience is an inner mechanism that guides our motives and choices towards honourable and correct conduct. It is calibrated to the level of the highest moral values and orientates us towards them. Rene Descartes named it *internal testimony*.

If we are in tune with our conscience, we are able to recognise its signals and make noble choices.

This mechanism communicates with us through feelings. When we feel good about our ideas and deeds, it would indicate that those are approved by our conscience. However, it is not necessarily a straightforward conclusion. For, if we feel uneasiness about the way we acted in a situation, it does not automatically mean that our behaviour was wrong – our fears and conditionings can overshadow our conscience.

Conscience leads human beings into cooperation and integration. It suggests selfless, loving, compassionate, and altruistic manners. Conscience can therefore be seen as an indicator of our moral sensibility.

Moral behaviour works to our evolutionary advantage. It cultivates a true human being in us, and provides our gradual ascension. This ascension adds strength to our physical cells, and steadily takes us towards the manifestation of our genetically programmed identity.

The human genetic programme is of cosmic origin, which means that the universal laws, the laws of natural equilibrium and divine justice are inherent in us. Our conscience is a mechanism perfectly aligned with these laws and it represents the voice of our genuine self. If we learn to discern and follow this voice, it will always show us the path that is congruent with our highest good.

HONESTY

Honesty involves adherence to the choices and behaviour that convey the truth.

It is most difficult to achieve honesty in relation to our own self, and to be able to genuinely recognise our strengths, weaknesses, needs or feelings. The role of honesty is to provide this capacity as well as to most correctly convey our truth in our communication with others. However, we are not to hurt other individuals by always insisting on expressing ourselves truthfully. Human interactions are about creating harmony, and a sense of unity and support.

Communicating the truth by the energies of our essence, such as respect, acceptance and humbleness, will potentially build a bridge made of essence-energy – which is the best pathway to exchange information or to cultivate a relationship on.

The power of honesty is immense. For, this vibration on its own can untangle some very complex energy knots, brought about by demanding situations or relationships. Thus honesty is a manifestation of wisdom and grows stronger as we recognise it. We do so by giving thanks to others for their honest behaviour and by sharing the truth of our essence. The more we pay attention to honesty, the more we spread it.

HUMBLENESS

Humility is an ability to restrain arrogance and pride by remaining modest. Though on a superficial level this behaviour might make us appear inferior, in fact, it is a manifestation of the true power of the character. A humble individual is capable of putting their own self below others. By lowering the value of personal achievements, humble people relativise self-importance regardless of who they are.

When we focus our attention, patience and support on others, communication becomes easy. In return, people love the company of a humble person, though they might not always be aware of the real reason for it. What surely attracts them to a humble person, is the space and attention they are given.

Humble people know their position in the world and have accepted it, hence they have no need to complain or show off. Those people are balanced and contented. They easily fit into any context.

GIVING

Humans usually have difficulty in choosing their best course of action. Many prefer to receive first and then, possibly, to give of themselves. Such an attitude seems to originate from an unconscious assumption of some kind of deficiency. People who entertain it, fail to notice that we always have enough to share and give – should we choose to do so. Their mind is still driven by self-interest and fear, which can lead them to disappointment.

True giving takes place before receiving, and without expecting anything in return. Such a giving is an expression of pure love. Since it conveys our essence-energy, it is more precious than the object or favour we give to somebody.

Giving can be accomplished by sharing our opinion, spiritual support, or material goods. Sometimes even a single world, a smile received, or a touch of a hand, can change the course of life of an individual. These simple human encounters add a crucial energy drop, needed to move things foreword.

Giving is an exercise of our heart, a test of its involvement in our affairs. Only a noble mind can adorn itself with the generosity of heart. Selfless giving, while helping others and contributing to their happiness, is the path to our genuine spiritual fulfilment. The more we give of ourselves to others, and to the world, the more goodness will come to us. The goodness we share keeps our essence-energy flowing, and the replenishing of it follows automatically.

What we give is equivalent to what we will receive. Inflicting pain and suffering on others will be balanced sooner or later, by us experiencing the same – otherwise we will have no chance to learn about the consequences of our behaviour. This balancing is regulated by a subconscious mechanism called *karma*. The mechanism of karma, reflects the universal laws as the ordinances of existence onto our coordinates.

Nobody inflicts on us pleasant or unpleasant situations, only we ourselves. To reach the level of a perfect human, we have to understand the impact of our behaviour on others, and learn to control it. Giving to other people the chance to be who they are, or forgiving them, is an act of significant spiritual maturity.

> *Misunderstandings are always caused by the inability of appreciating one another's point of view. – Nikola Tesla*

PLUGGING INTO MEANING

To conceive and convey meaning is a capacity specific to the consciousness of any level. Consequently, different people can assign different meanings to the same topic or situation.

Each meaning we discern is the result of harmonising our frequency with yet another frequency. After we determine the relevance of those new frequencies to us, a new quality is born. By integrating with ever higher number of frequencies, our awareness expands and grows towards an infinite awareness.

The frequencies we can resonate with are the "most meaningful" to us, and we embed them into our personal energy field. With each one of them, we acquire a new bit of the universe inside us.

Transcending "misunderstandings"

I did not mean that – is a sentence we often hear, which illustrates a collision of meanings due to the incongruent frequencies of two or more parties focused on the same subject.

Misunderstanding, as we call the collision of meaning, is a natural phenomenon we need to count on, and therefore not be surprised when we experience it. For example, each level of consciousness assigns a different meaning to the word *God* since each person accesses that notion from a different frequency. Nevertheless, each individual's understanding of God, as an authentic "version" of God, is equally plausible.

Thoughts are silent words. They can become spoken or written, or be expressed through an artwork or any other action. Beside the thought-chains which issue from our brain, brain energies can create mental pictures based on the same frequencies.

Not every word depicts the intended meaning. Hence the importance of learning and education: the more words we have a command of, the more equipped we are for determining and precise verbalisation of a meaning. A richer personal vocabulary therefore potentially reduces the probability of misunderstandings. However, the number of misunderstandings also decreases as we get to know our own selves more.

Knowing ourselves better is a glorious purpose we can work towards. During that process we add eternal values to the energy we epitomise. We integrate with the spiritual energy, which is our essence-energy and the backbone of our genetically predetermined godly personality. The current material reality and happenings on Earth are merely a training and testing medium, set up as a necessary stage towards the manifestation of our ultimate divine destiny.

We become more proficient in both distinguishing and conveying meaning, as our understanding of feelings and of the significance of all personal experience grows. The expansion of self-awareness is the expansion of the frequency range we operate through. Equally so, it is an expansion of all meanings relevant to us.

Whispering of our cells

Each cell of our body vibrates at a particular frequency. However, at the current level of human evolution on Earth, these vibrations are too subtle to be perceived. Hence they escape our attention and we cannot hear the messages our body is giving us.

Outside the human magnetic field, there is constant communication amongst the magnetic fields of stones, plants and animals. This communication is also beyond what we can consciously register. One day though, we will be able to decode the subtle sound vibrations coming both from our cells and from the world around us. When we purify ourselves enough and harmonise with those frequencies, we will "learn" the language they serve; and fully integrate with the realm of energies configured into what we call *nature*. By then, we might well drop the spoken/written word, and reorganise our memory, since our brain will acquire the power to access all information directly and immediately on demand.

The vibration that keeps an atom in an integrated whole is the vibration of love. Each entity in nature emanates this vibration. Hence the liveliness of plants and the innocence and purity of animals unmistakably exalts our spiritual being. We also feel great in the countryside or at the seaside, where the magnificence of the universal unconditional love reigns.

Nature does not contain the frequencies of human beings, or of their artefacts, but rather a frequency range from a depository of the Creator's wholesomeness and benevolence. For this reason, it is not the same to walk through a park, or through a wild forest or a meadow. The layout of the park, as well as the construction and maintenance of it, is the result of human mental and physical effort while a wild meadow and forest are, in that respect, free from human frequencies. In comparison to the beauty and tranquillity found in a park, nature's embrace is consequently richer and more revitalising.

Our planet is a cosmic library of creation pertaining to the mineral, plant and animal kingdoms. For that reason, the nature of Earth offers an unprecedented variety of experiences (frequencies) and potential inspiration to us.

We will truly integrate with nature when we reach the level of universal love and universal consciousness. The difference between our frequency and the frequency of nature will then diminish. Since we will also become unconditionally positive and loving, nature will seize on being the source of spiritual nourishment to us. Furthermore, our capacity to be inspired will not depend on our going out into a natural environment. We will reach deeper inner layers, and so the essence-source of both inspiration and spiritual power.

However, nature will not lose its significance to us and by then we will correct our relationship with it. Instead of exploiting and mistreating it as we still do, we will collaborate with nature, based on full respect and gratitude. Such human behaviour will signify the reaching of yet another level of meaning.

Nature is an aspect and product of cosmic *technology*[95] – the same as a human being. As we learn to solve the secrets of a human being, the discovering of the secrets of nature and cosmos will follow since we have all been designed using the same universal laws. These laws are automatically applied on Earth, as they are throughout the entire creation. They are superior to any man-made law and cannot be violated by human assumptions.

The universal laws govern not only what we consider to be the natural world but equally also the human social arena. Recognising these laws, and consciously applying them to all orders on our planet, will open a cosmic chapter of humanity's life on Earth.

Abstract meaning is not that abstract

Meaning is present in the planes beyond the reach of our awareness. Such meanings are inaccessible to us due to the limits of our current evolutionary level.

Our sentences are organised by meaning, and they exist to convey meaning. However, even at our evolutionary dimension, meaning also stretches beyond what words can successfully explain. Our feelings are one such example.

Feelings are not easily described and that is what gives an inspirational value and beauty to them. If our mind is to convey our feelings, through its rationality, it could distort their most authentic quality.

Our state of being is influenced by numerous factors such as our perceptions, thoughts, intuitions, desires, behavioural tendencies and previous experiences. Feelings are the result of this mélange and every moment are reflected onto our surroundings by our personal aura.

Due to the complexity of the factors that form a feeling, it is quite a task for our cognition to systematise them into a logical structure and evaluate them. Rather, it gives us great pleasure to weave the frequencies of our feelings into various artworks. In such a case, any attempt by the left brain hemisphere to describe them is bypassed.

The meaning behind our feelings continues to resonate through the art-form into which it has been imbued. Even the most abstract artworks are understood across cultures and independently of time, because they carry a meaning through the vibrations of the universal language, which is beyond words.

When I am tired of the insufficiency of words to describe meanings, I take brushes and paints and withdraw into silence. Each of my paintings is a visual record of the meanings I reach during those moments of deep quietness dedicated to colours.

Colours[96] are pure, neutral and endless – and they convey us into unknown realities, far beyond a canvas.

The more we open ourselves to essence of colours, the more we are ready to discover both about them and about ourselves. In that adventure of strolling through two infinities, we are rather unrestrained due to the neutrality of colours. For example, we could not say for the colour *red* that it is either good or bad. Hence in comparison to words, colours can never hurt us, even though they carry information through their own language. Intriguingly, they are both abstract and concrete at the same time.

Paintings are born through the personal frequency of their authors, yet each painting is accessible by people of all coordinates.

Every art-consumer re-creates the meaning of an artwork hence the grandness of art. It engages people by stimulating their imagination and by enabling them to have a pleasurable self-experience through new energies.

Artwork also works as a brain exercise, and as such it is a potential challenge to the consumer. When it comes to the acceptance of radically new meanings conveyed through art, society is not always ready to take them easily. The meanings of even highly abstract works of art may polarise opinions between social groups or individuals. One such polarisation led to breaking of the long friendship of two Dutch painters – Piet Mondrian and Theo Van Doesburg.

When Van Doesburg discovered Mondrian's work, focused on vertical and horizontal lines and the use of primary colours only, he was very inspired; and in the period 1915-1920 his paintings resembled Mondrian's.

However, after a break of four years, Van Doesburg returned to painting and decided to introduce diagonal lines, to make the composition more dynamic. Unfortunately, his great friend Mondrian was bitterly disappointed and could not take in this new approach. As a consequence, Mondrian terminated their friendship, and even rejected the whole avant-garde art movement *De Stijl* (*The Style* or *neoplasticism*) that Van Doesburg founded in 1917.

Every "little" change in painting style, such as introducing a diagonal into an orthogonal composition, is an artist's way of announcing new thoughts and meanings. It seems that famous Piet Mondrian was not ready for novel meanings and an inner transformation they required.

Another painter who lived in the same period, the Russian, Kazimir Malevich, has significantly stretched even the notion of *meaning* through his artwork. Malevich pioneered geometric abstract art in his country and around 1913 founded *suprematism* – an art movement focused on basic geometric forms, such as squares, circles and rectangles, painted in a limited range of colours. In 1915, as an established artist, he made breakthrough in his career, and in art in general, by exhibiting the painting *Black Square* (outlined with a white background). Absolute nonobjectivity led him to reach a profound philosophical meaning of white on a white background – hence he later painted *White on White* (a white square on a white background). That painting was another milestone in Malevich's work, in which he transcended the need to feature objects – hence he described both the background and the square by using one colour only. This ultimate minimalism signified the quintessence of suprematism – at which stage, to Malevich, visual objects, as the representation of the world and life, lost their meaning. The only thing that remained was the artist's being – and that very being communicated his experience through artwork. Malevich liberated himself from the efforts to construct-reconstruct the world in his paintings, and got closer to the "abstract" wealth of the universe – to the essence.

The delicate harmony of the universe is conveyed eloquently enough through the colour white on a white background only – according to the meanings that Malevich's consciousness conceived. What would be the difference between any amateur's production of the seemingly simplest possible artwork such as the painting of a white square on a white background and the painting *White on White* that Malevich presented? – It would be the depth of meaning given to these works by their authors. On a subtle energy level, as the imprint of their energy, authentic meaning dwells in the original paintings. Hence the painting *White on White* of Malevich carries this Russian artist's consciousness coordinates and the meaning he attributed to it. Observers access that meaning in proportion to their capacity to resonate with the frequencies Malevich embedded into this truly stupendous work of art.

Conquering new meanings – conquering the distances

The whole of existence converges on a primordial meaning assigned to it by its Creator. Every constituent of this endless performance therefore carries a divine purpose and meaning, and is programmed with the potential to fulfil it.

Our evolutionary trajectory is heading towards more advanced dimensions. In order to reach them, we need to acquire new meanings – rather than, by the use of space vehicles, conquer physical distances that separate evolutionary dimensions. In other words, landing on Saturn would not indicate that we have reached the evolutionary dimension of that planet. Until we are able to assimilate the frequencies of Saturn, biologically and through our consciousness, we will not truly ascend to the evolutionary medium of Saturn. Hence reaching other planets is not an adventure pertaining to visiting them, like we go to places of interest here, on Earth. Solving the evolutionary codes of those planets is only possible by the ascension of our consciousness, and therefore the realisation of new meanings.

We cannot inhabit a planet unless we have already completed our evolution through its energies.

Cosmic feasibility

The *Totality of Consciousness*[97] encompasses all forces, energies and knowledge – MEANINGFULLY woven into what is considered to be a neutral holistic Power. This Consciousness Totality certainly contains the four fundamental forces of nature identified by terrestrial science (gravity, electromagnetism, then strong and weak nuclear force) and so "recognises" them whether they are present within our brain (locally) or non-locally (somewhere in the myriad of the unified fields beyond Earth). The common factor in the interaction between those four fundamental forces, as well as the common factor in the interaction between the two fields, local and non-local, is MEANING.

In the manifestation processes (of a personal wish, for example) the multidimensional alignment of meanings is also important. The mental pictures produced by our brain act like a prescription: a local field suggests or, perhaps, invites the macro planes to collaborate in a project on the particular coordinates of a given person.

Higher planes hold the meanings that extend beyond the perceptual and cognitive capacity of the lower planes. The meanings of the higher planes are invisible templates of possibilities. For this reason, without complying with the laws and orders of the higher planes, a wish of the lower plane is destined to remain unfulfilled. This is like going to your boss to ask for holiday. The boss will know whether the wish is feasible. Hence the holiday will happen or not, depending on whether one's absence at a particular time is also acceptable (meaningful) at the level administered by the boss. Alignment of meaning is necessary for any agreement and manifestation.

Intention

Intention cannot exist without meaning, but only a single mental picture is enough to capture that meaning. Mental pictures are a result of brain power to embed the frequency of meaning into the brain cells. This local event is reported to the higher planes by the very frequency of its meaning.

The bridge between our mental pictures (wishes) and their physical manifestation is the frequency of the meaning they share. No wonder the instructions on how to make one's wishes come true consistently suggest visualisation. However, visualisation is not the sole factor that will lead to manifestation because no human's wish or power can interfere with the execution of the universal laws.

People can mentally and deliberately influence some processes within the physical world, such as induce *healing*[98] by consciously modulating rhythms of the brain waves. However, can we develop a power to govern the way the forces of nature interact, and make them constantly succumb to our intentions? Nikola Tesla firmly believed that was where the true future of human beings was to be found – earned by purification, self-disciplining and spiritual empowerment. Such a future belongs to those individuals who are fully cognisant of the supremacy of the natural (universal) laws and apply them to enhance social wellbeing.

Boredom is due to the lack of meaning

The ability to conceive a meaning is parallel to our capacity to produce mental models founded upon the frequencies that we can constructively relate to. In our environment, we continuously go through the process of assessing the frequencies of objects, living beings, and nature, or of the situations that we are exposed to. At the current level of human evolution, unfortunately, we can harmonise with only some of those frequencies.

In all encounters we experience, our primary challenge is to preserve our inner balance (internal system) – an inner peace. At some point, however, we become aware of the importance of supporting the wellbeing of external systems too. Gradually then, we learn to harmonise with other individuals and the rest of the world. We cannot be truly happy unless we are successful in both of these arenas – internal and external.

People who are bored suffer from an incapacity to function comfortably within either of these energy networks. These people are unable to find a valuable enough meaning in any frequency/energy, in order to be motivated and go into action. Nothing seems attractive to them – because the attraction power of their thought is low and their subtle energy field, known as their aura, is weak. Our personal aura is a map that connotes the total of our cellular and mental vibrations, and it is built in proportion to our positive thoughts. Hence if bored people dwell on negative thoughts, they drastically deplete their already weak aura.

Bored people are a drag not only on the environment but on their own selves. By keeping the scope of frequencies they comfortably operate through as very narrow, these people deprive themselves of vital interactions that enhance both human body and mind, and contribute to our evolutionary processes.

Biologists have discovered that the vitality of an energy node, in the network of our metabolic processes, is in direct proportion to the number of connections the node maintains with other nodes. The pathways between these miniature stations are like streams of energy that comes to stimulate them. The same principle applies to a star, or a universe. Their power (a unified field) is increased as more lights, of colossal speeds, reach them. The human being is empowered in the same way – through the multiplicity of interactions.

Meeting of complex meanings

When two people meet for the first time, at a party or during a train journey, two sets of holistic energies spontaneously start to relate. This automatic process beyond our awareness involves the investigation of a possible alignment of frequencies. If sufficient compatibility is detected through this unconscious scanning, the attraction power leads the two people into an explicit communication.

The significance of the meeting will much depend on the overlapping of frequencies between the two of them (common meanings). Hence, they might continue to see one another occasionally or even commit to spend the rest of their lives together, by loyally and self-sacrificingly building the meaning of their togetherness. In any case, our relationships reflect our ability to transcend self-importance, and each one of them is a precious opportunity to advance our own meaning.

The more friends and colleges we communicate with, the stronger the network of meaning we function through. Our evolutionary aptitude is therefore higher, because we are capable of harmonising with a bigger number of vibrations around us. Hence highly successful individuals in whatever arena are powerful energies, able to handle very complex and demanding energy networks.

To agree on the same meaning is a huge evolutionary challenge for two or more people who intend to gather around a common idea. An endeavour to find and maintain a mutually acceptable meaning, among the number of people, signifies their realisation that power is born from unity. Such people are aware that they will achieve less if remain isolated, on the level of individual aspirations. Human beings getting together is an evolutionary necessity, not only from the point of physical survival but for the sake of their spiritual development too.

There is an immense beauty in togetherness, despite all the challenges involved. Once we discover it, we become like busy spiders building wide networks of contacts, projects and social interactions – even beyond those necessary for securing our financial survival. Our ability to update knowledge and hold new visions then steadily grows. However, in our socialising, it will always be a common meaning that we will need to recognise in each situation, in order to keep us fully present and vibrant.

Frequency of meaning is chosen by the observer

To expand the understanding of our own selves requires mastering new frequencies. Hence every experience has great value since it exposes us to our own selves in a new context.

Relating to others also necessitates openness towards new frequencies and readiness to harmonise with them. In other words, socialising enhances our personal meaning. Each new frequency adopted, also adds power to our power.

If one still has unresolved issues with anybody on this planet, particularly with members of their own family, it indicates that such a person has not found a meaning to some frequencies that are important to them. Those people are distressed due to their incapacity to harmonise their personal energy with particular frequencies. Hence they fail to empower themselves with yet another vibrational quality of the life-force.

Our negative attitudes assign a negative meaning to some events, behaviour or words. Interestingly, somebody else may see them through a positive attitude. Obviously, these two opposite approaches ascribe different qualities to the same events. Those qualities are the frequency of meaning, relevant to the observer and chosen by the observer. We are given the freedom and the capacity to make these choices. In the process of applying this freedom, we learn – even about the implications of freedom.

Excessive exposure to the frequencies that carry negative meaning is damaging to our health. Besides, by taking a negative attitude, we live in a distorted reality due to our observation point not being neutral. It is good to have in mind that the Creator is a Totality of Neutral Consciousness, and therefore to strive to reach neutrality in every situation.

Neutrality is a most energy efficient way of existing. It avoids any waste of energy through judging, non-accepting or holding to one's opinions and their intensities. It is the ticket to effortless flow. In fact, neutral consciousness is the peak of our evolution hence is not easy to reach it.

Each meaning is a colour

Colours carry information through their specific frequency. Those frequencies are also transmitted through sounds.

Each frequency possesses a meaning hence the issuing of a meaning is equivalent to evoking a particular colour or uttering a sound. Positive and negative attitudes are carried by different colours since they represent different meanings.

Reasoning, infused by meaning, emanates colours – whether we talk or just think. Thoughts (sentences) are a stream of colours and our speeches are complex paintings.

At the higher universal dimensions, the colour-sound-light is an integrated power. Black represents such a power.

Black is the most saturated colour medium composed primarily of 49 (7x7) colours while, interestingly, universal singe musical note has *49 (7x7) sound aspects*[99]. All colours merge in the medium of black hence the *colour black*[100] acts as a depository of infinite knowledge (meanings). Infinite awareness is also the domain of black. Nikola Tesla stated the *black* is the true face of light.

Frequency of meaning

A tulip, a stone, a human, are each a complex arrangement of energies with distinctive properties (meaning) in the chain of energies. In different languages, these words (tulip, stone, human) are composed of different letters hence their letter frequencies are not identical. However, the frequency of their meaning is the same in every language. Letter frequencies are mastered by learning a language, while the understanding of meanings depends on the consciousness level of an individual.

If it was not for meaning, we would not be able to translate words from one language to another – because what we transfer between the languages is meaning. For the success of any human interaction, the precision in expressing meaning is also crucial. Clarity is therefore a great asset. It is a precious time and energy saver.

Human communication is not just about us being sincere in exposing our stance. It is equally about making a conscious effort to invest in harmony. Hence tailoring our interactions according to each situation and showing intent to support harmony, would be a great contribution that we could make towards building the culture of respect, order and beauty. This realisation in itself is yet another layer of meanings pertaining to the socialisation processes of human beings.

Meaning of a moment

What gives meaning to every moment in our life? – It is the totality of energies present on the planet, refracted through our personal frequency prism. Our changing thoughts, feelings and intentions influence the resulting colour/meaning of every second of our life.

Does the falling of an old tree, in a far away forest, have any meaning for us?

Even if we do not witness something, it does not exclude the fact that that phenomenon has a meaning in the context of our operational domain – though beyond our awareness. Life is an immaculate programme in which all constituents contribute to its success. It is the programme where the ultimate Singularity exercises its integrity and meaning through the plurality of self-aspects. So, unwitnessed phenomena, such as the collapsing of an old tree in a forest or the wing-flapping of the Monarch-butterflies in America, add their vibrations to the planetary energy field and so are woven into the life medium of Earth. Though minute, in comparison to the energy we experience in our direct daily interactions with other people, these influences are real.

Nikola Tesla illustrated this phenomenon by saying that somebody might suddenly become sad, and struggle to understand the causes behind it. However, Tesla explained, the person could then figure out that in the instance of the mood change one cloud had covered the sun.

Numerically coded meanings

Perfect seal

The Existential Programme is a template of meanings given to the frequencies (energies), by the Creator. In this programme, within the Dimension of Time and Space, the *7x7 evolutionary trajectory*[101] structures the evolutionary (frequency) scales of energy, form and consciousness.

For example, there are 7 main stages pertaining to the development of the physical form used by an *evolving energy*[102]. Each of these stages progresses through 7 phases. The evolving energy experiences these steps by incarnating through a chain of forms within mineral-plant-animal kingdoms thus advancing towards the organisms with a more complex brain structure and towards light. Eventually, it deserves to evolve by using a human body.

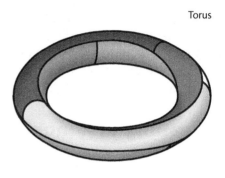

Torus

Human consciousness and brain also evolve through 7 stages, till the individual reaches the level of human perfection, defined by the Creator. Interestingly, our body is composed of 7 subtle bodies, a light-universe is made of 7 light-universes, a rainbow has 7 main colours (at our evolutionary level), and a musical scale has 7 notes ordered by their fundamental frequencies.

"Star of David"

Further still, a surface of a doughnut-like three-dimensional shape, in geometry known as a *torus*, can be divided into a maximum of 7 regions so that *every* one of them touches the other 6 regions only once. If these regions are coloured by different colours, each colour will touch the remaining 6 colours one time only. This is a property unique to the torus – among all three-dimensional forms. Due to its exclusive characteristics, torus is considered a prototype of black/white holes and other celestial phenomena.

Ring of Solomon

The *Seal of Solomon* (or *Ring of Solomon*), attributed to King Solomon (10th century BC), was venerated in medieval Islamic cultures and in Western esoteric practices. In the Jewish tradition the same figure is known as the *Star of David*. According to the legends of Arabic medieval writers, this ring carried an engraved name of God and was given to Solomon, directly from Heaven. Hence Solomon was able to command demons and speak to animals. In order to restrict access to the magic power of this ring, later on, its initial geometry of a *six-pointed star*[103] was veiled by inscribing 7 circles of equal size in it – hence the figure called the *perfect seal* appeared.

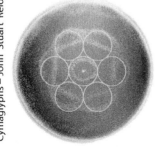

Cymaglyphs – John Stuart Reid

Interestingly, the cymaglyph pattern behind the vibration of the letter (sound) "O" resembles the geometry of the *perfect seal*.

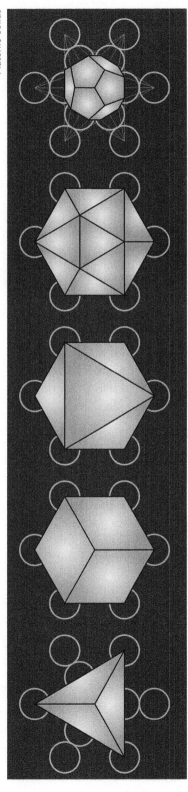

The cymaglyphs are images of reproducible patterns, obtained through the study of sounds. These images reveal the relation between sound (vibration) and the configuring of material form.

With the development of acoustics, we could understand more easily the well-known sentence featured in both *Far East Philosophies* and the sacred books that states: *In the beginning was the Word, and the Word was with God and the Word was God.* Unequivocally, this sentence indicates that sound is a power instrumental to the process of physical manifestation.

How significant then is the geometry behind the *Solomon Seal* (and the sound O) – if the *Ring of Solomon* stands for the name of God? Does it mean that "O" is one of the names of God? And what does the recurrence of the number 7, in the above mentioned instances, tell us?

Obviously, there is a consistency in the design of the entire creation carried by particular numbers. These numbers are the unchanging keys of the essential formations.

Numbers live in geometries and so, disguised, parade before our eyes. For example, the *perfect seal* figure shows the presence of the number 7 in hexagonal geometry. This figure also illustrates the fractal quality of a circle.

Intriguingly, the hexagonal web is the template that preserves the proportions of *Platonic solids* (tetrahedron, cube, octahedron, dodecahedron and icosahedron). As archetypal three-dimensional shapes, these solids are fundamental blocks of the entire creation.

Webs of meanings are sustained by various agents. Numbers are one of them.

MISSION-CONSCIOUSNESS

Contexts are interminable

There is one common role of everything in existence: to support the order of the Totality by acting on specific coordinates. Is a human being exempt from this order? – Highly unlikely. The purpose of our life therefore exists, even before we become aware of what it is.

Hence, each individual's universal mission is to discover, within the existential dimension they find themselves in, the divine order and then to fit into that order by consciously serving it.

Would it really be possible to produce a life programme in which some elements would not have any function or purpose at all? In a design of a building, would an architect determine a space or any structural element to exist for their own sake – outside the plurality of functions within the building? Similarly, does a computer game designer include meaningless characters or details in the game? Even if an author would declare as "meaningless" certain elements of his design, those elements will automatically gain a meaning (and that is – *to be meaningless*). For, everything that comes into existence is infused with a meaning – without the frequency of meaning it will not transpire on the tapestry of life.

Each constituent in life, no matter how minute or gigantic, serves its purpose within the context in which it exists. Contexts are innumerable and they are scaled throughout the creation. They are nested within more complex systems and so on, till the total of *All-There-Is*. This Absolute Singularity is called various names such as *God, Totality of Consciousness, unified field, the creation,…* all depending on the observational glasses – whether they belong to a spiritually, scientifically or philosophically inclined person. Nevertheless, as the human consciousness expands, the understanding and the boundaries of this Totality inevitably expand too.

> *What we now want most is closer contact and better understanding between individuals and communities all over the earth and the elimination of that fanatic devotion to exalted ideals of national egoism and pride, which is always prone to plunge the world into primeval barbarism and strife. – Nikola Tesla*

Voluntary work

Humans are never given impossible tasks by the Creator. Also, the solution of a very complex and challenging situation is often found in the simplicity of the

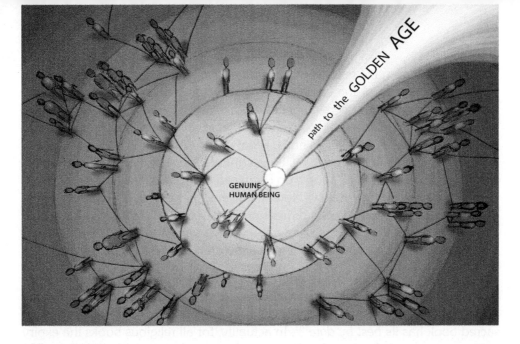

common sense avenue. Unfortunately, common sense is not that commonly applied, for it requires a profound alignment of a mind with the highest universal signals.

What would happen if even a single cell stopped working in a human body? Though minute, the absence of one cell's functional contribution will gradually reflect on the particular organ it belongs to, then on the whole body, and potentially it will endanger the life of the person. For the wellbeing of society, a mutual support amongst individuals is equally important because each one of us is like a single cell within the totality of a Single Being.

There are many ways to become useful to society and consciously support it. However, as well as the paid modalities there is a whole plethora of voluntary engagements. The difference between the two is big. Voluntary work comes from nobility of the individual who has the inner clarity that they already live in abundance. Such an individual wants to share time, enthusiasm, skills and emotional support, with those temporarily less fortunate and so help them get better and happier.

Prior to the path of social integration and philanthropic deeds, we experience ourselves through the competitiveness of a dualistic consciousness.

Unifying despite all differences

What were the sacred books telling us behind their elaborate narratives? By introducing the notion of Heaven, have they not been hinting at a blissful community of human beings, suggesting GOD (Love of GOD and a humble obedience to His Will) as a unification factor? If so, how far in that direction have we progressed?

The sacred books have managed to unite people under their teachings, though within the followers of the same sacred books some divisions have occurred. However, despite these segregations, no other celestial programme applied on our planet within the last 6000 years has gathered millions of people at the same coordinates as the sacred books have. What is obviously left to do now is to stop animosities and wars that have religious connotations (as well as other origins) so that the unification of all people on Earth can take place – regardless of which, if any, sacred book they follow. How might that be possible? – By completing evolution through the Religious dimension first; because people who have truly gained a religious education, tolerate both atheists and those educated through different sacred books and do not impose their religious creeds on others.

Religious education is an evolutionary path through a specific range of energies (frequencies). These energies have been necessary for the evolution of human beings at particular stages during a specific period. In other words, it is as if *every* sacred book has its *best by date*[104]. In actuality, for all religious books the expiry date on our planet, foreseen by the celestial authorities, was the end of the 20th century.

By the year 2000, those living on Earth were to become saturated with the frequency of the sacred texts (the 18th Evolutionary dimension), and as such to be ready to move on to evolution through the universal knowledge beyond religions (19th Evolutionary dimension). At the beginning of the 20th century, the building of the foundation of the Golden Age on our planet started, though the blossoming of this new Lordly Order will begin in the 23rd century.

When worshipping rituals are performed, one attains an extraordinarily positive state of being where even the slightest negativities do not exist. Since our aura is supported by our positive thoughts, the process of worshiping suggested by the sacred books has provided a mechanism for the continuous strengthening of human beings with the energies delivered to Earth by those books.

Religious *worshipping*[105] is a divine prescription. It aims at disciplining, purifying and *evolving* humans through specific vibrations. The ritual prayer positions, suggested in the Islamic sacred book, stimulate some inner organs and so add to physical wellbeing of the follower.

The energy spectrum of the sacred books facilitates the growth of human consciousness towards a level of religious fulfilment. When that stage is reached, *prayers*[106] do not work anymore. In other words, prayers cannot attract energy from beyond the Religious dimension. Hence the energy of the Universal dimension, which then becomes an evolutionary requirement, escapes those who continue practising religious rituals.

After the point of religious fulfilment, the source of necessary evolutionary energy changes and evolvement through learning the explicit universal truths commences. From the alpha energy of the Religious dimension, one therefore shifts to the evolutionary nourishment with the beta energy from the Universal dimension. Even though it is a new evolutionary path, it is assisted by the same celestial authorities who have revealed each sacred book to our planet. It is the path of those who can accept one another, and join in the programme of universal unification reflected on Earth.

Only by unconditionally and equally valuing each human being, can we step into a proper global unification. If we fully understand that planetary peace and prosperity are in the best interest of each country, of each nation, of each individual – it means we are able to hear our essence-logic. Hence, sooner or later, we will find enough goodwill to pursue that direction.

Mission-consciousness is encoded into our genes

Mission-consciousness is our universal duty. It is encoded in our genes and programmed to be activated at a particular stage of our evolvement. At the base of this consciousness are virtues such as responsibility, respect, sense of unity – all delivered through self-sacrifice. At that level, the collective interest is placed before the individual interests and wishes. Thus the universal mission-consciousness comes after an individual transcends their personal self-importance. Such an individual is able to find meaning in a selfless investing of their energy, knowledge and time, into a future of peace and unity. Hence, they will work wholeheartedly to support this planet and the universe.

The choice of voluntary organisation that one will establish or join, might change over time. Eventually, the human essence will recognise the godly path beyond religions, and engage in its universal mission.

Our mission-consciousness gets activated when our evolving consciousness matches the specifics of the time-energy that we experience. Only then do we really tune into the time we live in, and so can utilise time-energy! It is as if we previously existed as anachronous organisms, disconnected from the energy values of our life medium. With this fine alignment we become ready for a universal mission; hence such a mission can transpire on our path. From the moment of embarking on that mission, a conscious participation in the orders of the universe becomes an imperative for the happiness of an entity. For, any underperforming, pertaining to our capacity or our evolutionary level, creates a medium of dissatisfaction.

Just as everything is subject to deserving, so this applies to our mission-consciousness.

Matter of deserving

According to the universal laws, nothing is offered to us unless we are ready for the intensity of the energy behind it. This means that, every single moment, our evolvement is evident to the powers that govern the Existential Programme.

In the universal archives there is a record of all our past lives and all our thoughts that were ever conceived. These records are updated on daily bases by the mediation of UFOs[145] and huge mother-ships. These spaceships relay collected data (our thought-chains aggregated over each 24-hour segment) to its final celestial destination for safekeeping and analytical purposes. Hence, even though we forget our thoughts, the universe "remembers" them because it stores them on our personal diskettes in its computers.

Consequently, the celestial realm knows each one of us, and therefore Earth's human beings, better than we do. Thus, subject to our capacity (*deserving*), it measures the dosages of energies sent to our planet aiming to produce the best evolutionary results.

However, sometimes it seems that we are loaded with more than we could cope with. When we think this way, we fail to recognise that all circumstances have always been a reflection of the universal laws, and the technology of advanced dimensions, onto the existential plane of Earth – and thus are by no means random or erroneous.

Deserving, and what transpires in our life, are never a direct product of personal wishes. For, *to deserve* means to be able to deal with the energy of anticipated situation. Hence *deserving* clearly pertains to the laws of physics.

If the Creator orchestrates His Is-ness aiming at the prosperous maintenance of the Self, then the Existential Programme fundamentally stimulates our progress not our deterioration. Our experiences, whether they are pleasant or unpleasant, are therefore ultimately a result of the Creator's intents manifested at our coordinates – hence they are divinely approved as *deserved*. Regarding the events we do not go through: we are either not yet ready for their frequencies or within our cells we have already recorded the frequencies related to those experiences – as a learnt lesson.

No individual can rightly assess this subject since here, on Earth, we are unfolding a fully automated celestial programme that, as such, is beyond the reach of human beings. Nevertheless our evolutionary needs are continuously assisted by the application of the ordinance of graduality, which *deserving* is all about.

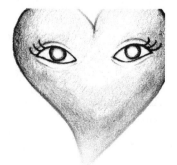

The truth of our origin and of our purpose is one

Human life on Earth has reached the 21st century AD, after millennia long investments of the celestial realm in that direction. Due to the universal laws and the programme of evolution, we come across and experience only that what we need to – not necessarily what we would want to. Our progress follows the objectives of the energy that we epitomise.

Evolutionary frequency is exclusive to each human being, and belongs to a specific dimension. Hence the personal colour of every individual is unique; their personal sound vibration is unique. However, our purpose is common to all energies and that is *to serve the orders of the universal totality*. To become conscious of this is an evolutionary achievement and equally so a privilege. Humans on our planet have been prepared *en masse* to henceforth reach that stage of evolvement.

The truth of our origin and of our purpose is one. Becoming aware of life beyond our village, city, country, planet, galaxy and so on, gets us closer to that truth. Only by comprehending our cosmic origin, can we be confident in discerning our true life-mission.

Even though we currently live on Earth, the truth as to *who we are* and *why we are here* is of a context that surpasses the physical boundaries and destiny of this planet.

Maturity of heart

Participating in a mission that involves the uniting of humanity on Earth, and within the universe, is available only from certain level of evolvement. As with everything, it is a matter of divine timing, pertaining to the evolution of an individual. Hence, it is not offered before we are ready.

The *universal mission*[107] sprouts from the maturity of our heart: evolved enough to bear the distracting tendencies of a chattering mind, and to expose its own logic against it. The maturity of heart is fundamental to integration processes in the entire universe.

People of a mature heart selflessly support the entire creation from within their particular evolvement dimension. They feel a genuine gratitude merely for the opportunity to come into existence and to perpetuate their own life programmes. They are happy with who they are and what they have, because they are aware of how everything can unfavourably change in one instant and how our most valuable possessions, the inner ones, have been earned by the aeons-long efforts of an evolving energy.

The individuals, who serve the creation from this consciousness level, act from their essence. They are able to relativise their own significance, and seemingly become nonexistent due to giving priority to the needs of other people, society and the Divine Order. However, through that very service the most humane aspects of our persona are activated, such as self-sacrificing, humility, compassion, acceptance and tolerance. Living out those values consolidates the magnificence of our being.

> I strongly believe in the rule of compensation. True awards are always in proportion with work and sacrifices. – Nikola Tesla.

Unity-consciousness

On the map of the creation, our planet is not even that big as a dust particle, yet our existence makes an impact on the formation of the new soul-seeds, and therefore of the new worlds and universes. As well as the cosmic significance of each human, the importance of every single particle of energy is also paramount since all energy is heading toward more evolved forms. A single particle is on its way to becoming a human being and then godlike, by manifesting full human genetic potential (essence-consciousness). Even though humans can create wonders, unfortunately, with a certain mind-set, a single person can destroy the entire planet – hence the evolution of human beings is fully supervised by the celestial authorities.

Perfect human beings dwell in the unity-consciousness nourished by their essence. They have transcended the duality-consciousness that primarily operates by classifying the perceptions and experiences in a confrontational manner, while emphasising the differences. Unity-consciousness focuses on the commonality of elements in each situation and tends to create harmony in a win-win manner, where there are no so-called *losers*. As such, this consciousness mode relates to the right brain hemisphere.

On the path of unity-consciousness, responsibility, self-sacrifice, sense of duty and acceptance, are *tested*[108] to the utmost – not as adopted concepts but through the way we behave. Submission to Divine Orders and eagerness to contribute to the wellbeing of others, are evident from our readiness to adopt self-sacrifice.

Mission-consciousness is the path of light and cannot exist without the virtue of self-sacrificing. Those who establish their own family, and particularly when they become parents, open a programme of thorough training for mission-consciousness.

Mission-consciousness is based on love in which heart and mind are loyal partners.

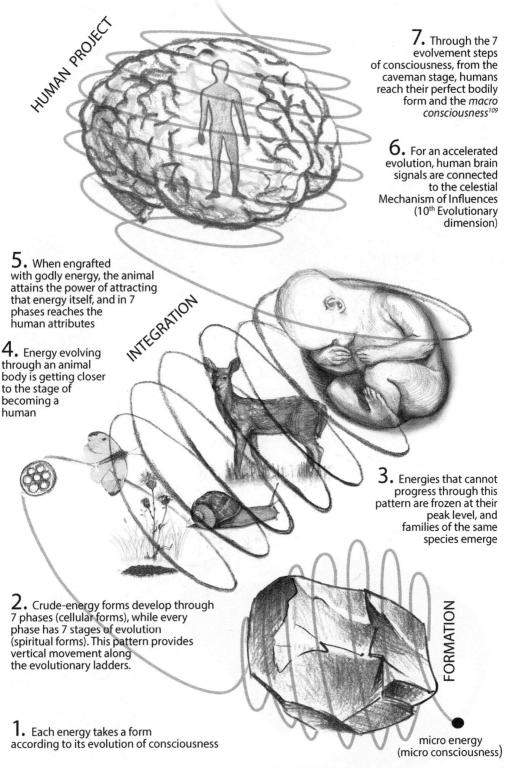

HUMAN PROJECT

7. Through the 7 evolvement steps of consciousness, from the caveman stage, humans reach their perfect bodily form and the *macro consciousness*[109]

6. For an accelerated evolution, human brain signals are connected to the celestial Mechanism of Influences (10th Evolutionary dimension)

5. When engrafted with godly energy, the animal attains the power of attracting that energy itself, and in 7 phases reaches the human attributes

INTEGRATION

4. Energy evolving through an animal body is getting closer to the stage of becoming a human

3. Energies that cannot progress through this pattern are frozen at their peak level, and families of the same species emerge

2. Crude-energy forms develop through 7 phases (cellular forms), while every phase has 7 stages of evolution (spiritual forms). This pattern provides vertical movement along the evolutionary ladders.

FORMATION

1. Each energy takes a form according to its evolution of consciousness

micro energy (micro consciousness)

CRUDE MATTER FORMS

7

FITTING INTO
COLLECTIVE FIELD

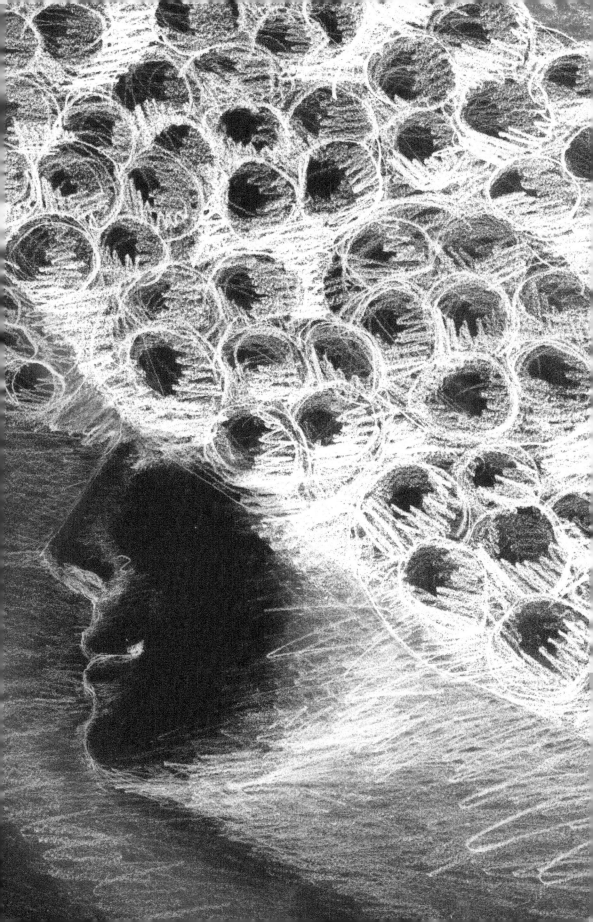

SCIENCE AND RELIGION

Necessity of belief

From the moment they emerged within our planetary society, science and religion have been addressing the questions of the origins of life and of humanity. Though they share the same objective, their starting premises and methods used are different. Due to an unshakable commitment to their respective stances, religion and science have managed to survive the teasing of one another for millennia, and unfortunately have not yet found any means to constructively merge into one truth.

Science does not accept anything as a truth unless that phenomenon has been sieved through scientific methodology and fully complies with the scientific principles. Scientists use experiments, measuring, analyses, and predominantly an operational mode of the left brain hemisphere.

On the other hand, religion suggests that ultimate truths belong to a transcendental medium, and are independent of our ability to experience them. Emanuel Kant, the 18th-century German philosopher, claimed that a human being possessed inherent cognitive faculties to enable knowledge, justification or argument prior to any particular experience. This "inner knowledge" closely relates to pure belief.

Belief is a fruit of the right brain hemisphere. This part of brain processes data in a holistic manner, intuitively, creatively, and is capable of deriving meaning from seemingly unrelated elements.

All religious doctrines were propagating faith as a bridge to the spiritual source. However, faith is necessary for our development even beyond its application in the religious context. It is not a fear-generated or blind faith, but a conscious faith.

> *There is no pleasure in science without hope, and as long as a man lives without ideals, he remains unhappy. Religious is one noble ideal, and it seems that great reformers, who had set the rules of conduct long time ago, were right in their conclusions saying a peaceful existence and continuous progress of a man were essentially dependent on the concept of God*
>
> *– Nikola Tesla*

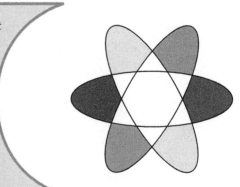

Merging two paths

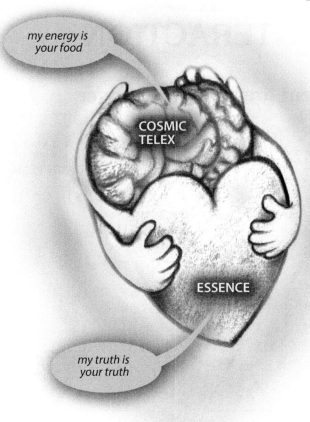

Science can discover many things relating to the creation but will never be able to prove the God-Creator with its methods. The reason is simple – if God was provable through the capacity of a terrestrial or any other mind or through technology, He would not then be that single A B S O L U T E (ESSENCE) POWER behind the entire creation. However, science will move closer to understanding and describing this Power as the very embodiment of reality, when it steps firmly into what is considered spiritual and supernatural.

In the religious arena though, believers FEEL a connection to God and have no need to rationally explain that experience – nor do they seek a scientific validation in order to accept God's actuality.

In advanced dimensions, science and religion are integrated into a single knowledge, yet at our evolutionary coordinates on Earth they are two separate learning avenues. If science and religion are to reach the universal truths on the origin of energy, matter, life and humanity, their conclusions must be the same – since there is only one universal truth pertaining to the genesis of the entire creation.

The triumph of humanity will be when these two complementary evolvement paths join forces. That milestone will signify a meeting of physics and metaphysics, intellect and heart. The existential truth, accepted by both scientists and believers, will therefore become one.

The truth of the rational mind will then become the truth of the loving heart.

TRUTH IS REACHED THROUGH INTERACTION

Earth and firmament are linking stronger

The universal truth is present in our genes. To animate that potential, a human seed is stimulated throughout numerous lifetimes by the use of necessary energies. These energies are projected onto our planet by a celestial reflection system of *prismatic pathways[110]*. What is reflected are energy particles of a specific quality, tailored to the level of consciousness on our planet at any given time. These cosmic rains are a source of information, as well as a connective factor between Earth and the celestial realms.

The cosmic energy we receive links us back to the cosmic depths, in which our older brothers and sisters reside. As our ability to utilise this energy grows, Earth and *firmament[111]* are bonding ever more strongly. This link is very real, and is a part of the truth of who we are. However, for millennia this fact has been escaping our attention.

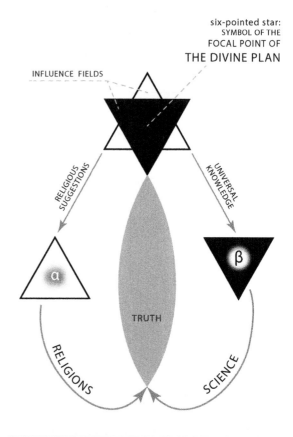

six-pointed star: SYMBOL OF THE FOCAL POINT OF THE DIVINE PLAN

INFLUENCE FIELDS

RELIGIOUS SUGGESTIONS

UNIVERSAL KNOWLEDGE

α

β

TRUTH

RELIGIONS

SCIENCE

> *The day science begins to study non-physical (spiritual) phenomena, it will make more progress in one decade than in all the previous centuries of its existence.*
> – Nikola Tesla.

What is the truth?

This question is perhaps as old as humankind's ability to think.

Is there more than one truth on each topic and, if so, how do we agree on which one to accept for individual and social application?

There is a truth of cosmic origin and significance, based on the fundamental *universal laws*[112]. Everything in existence is subject to those laws. Even blooming of a flower or coming of a storm, are manifestations of these predetermined orders.

What we call *chance* does not exist in the chain of life; each circumstance is a medium prepared according to the universal laws. Consequently, every single meeting of two people is celestially arranged – to happen at the best time and place; and for the necessary outcomes to be achieved with the least use of energy.

Having seeded the life on Earth, having evolved it to the current human level, the *supreme realms*[113] apply universal laws on our planet as well as on all other planets and galaxies. Some of these laws relate to nature and some to governing. The entities that become conscious of the universal laws respect them genuinely, and through a conscious service, outlined by these very laws, express their appreciation to the Creator.

The one truth, contained in the universal laws, is interpreted through countless understandings of it by human beings functioning on various coordinates. These coordinates are consciousness level coordinates. Since the coordinates are different for each person, perception of the same reality is inevitably coloured by the individual's evolvement stage, and thus each person is the possessor of a unique view and experiences pertaining to the same subject. All the observations are correct. However, for a happy life, we need to agree on common truths, which are closest ones to the universal laws – otherwise we will remain on the individualistic, antagonistic and separatist plane of a dualistic consciousness.

Reality on Earth is changing so rapidly as if the process of a global blood transfusion is taking place. The planetary living medium is being fortified with stronger energy, unknown to us, which carries new information and truth from the higher planes of the universe. Hence all human beings and their terrestrial establishments are affected, yet the majority of the population is unaware of the origin and the purpose of the pressure that life on Earth is now putting on us. However, everybody feels that life is not as it used to be – even only a few years ago.

The new cosmic energies, acting as new blood, are mercilessly demanding changes. However painful some of those changes might seem, their final result is to our advantage.

Individual truths need to be increasingly relativised, and passed through the prism of universal energy/knowledge for assessment and further validation – in order to reflect the lasting quality of the universal standards.

Fitting into a group

Humans are social beings. Nevertheless, we first need to develop a sense of individuality and then transcend it in order to become successful in a social context. We therefore learn to be humble and to find a constructive position within a group and a wider social arena.

Living and interacting with other individuals and with our environment is crucial for unfolding of our genetic programme. One path determined by our genetic code makes us acquire physical skills such as to walk, talk, run or sing. This path is lived on an instinctive level, and is supported by our social environment.

The other *evolvement path*[114], encoded into our genes, is an educational path that provides the development of our consciousness. Thought is crucial for the activation of, and success, on this path, yet without our social interactions even our consciousness will not evolve properly. Hence, social hermits put in danger their emotional and social intelligence, as well as their personality development in general. If a child is severely deprived of social interaction, it would suffer stunted development and so could remain a *tabula rasa*.

We have become who we are today, due to the development of our consciousness on this second evolvement path.

A rich social network is ideal for many aspects of our evolution, because each social interaction can help us to understand who we are. In that evolutionary process, the aim is to see, and to treat as ourselves, every person we encounter. For, we are one body of humanity, and we share the same origin and the same evolutionary objective – regardless of all specific attributes of our persona or our social group. The differences between us serve as precious polishing agents. By experiencing them, we witness our own self within the flow of human energies and thus our spiritual maturity is continuously tested.

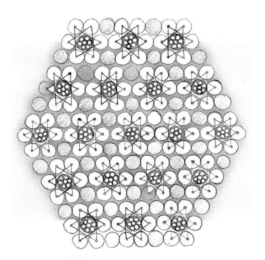

The truth of our evolutionary level is evident through our behaviour. Current planetary circumstances reflected on our local environment, are a highly challenging energy mixture that we experience on daily basis. Furthermore, every single event we encounter is an energy setup, divinely modelled as an exam. Events therefore present us with an opportunity to integrate a particular energy into our biology, and move on towards human perfection.

infinity

EVOLUTION of CONSCIOUSNESS

level of consciousness

level of consciousness

MENTAL PATH

social network

THOUGHT

VOLUME of AWARENESS

walking

running

cycling

singing

swimming

PHYSICAL SKILLS

INSTINCTIVE DEVELOPMENT

BEHAVIOUR

*But instinct is something which transcends knowledge.
We have, undoubtedly, certain finer fibres that enable us to perceive truths
when logical deduction, or any other willful effort of the brain, is futile. – Nikola Tesla.*

Family is an evolutionary institution

Transcending the viewpoint of an individualistic consciousness is an ability acquired through evolution. It takes one's awareness through the stages – Me, Me-You, Us – as the stances to operate from.

The Me-level is primarily concerned with personal needs and wishes, and rather ignores the rest of the world. We can observe it in the cases of children and some very old people. It is a natural attitude, necessary for the protection of those least independent and most vulnerable.

The Me-You level takes the other person into consideration too. It makes a clean distinction between the two sets of interests, yet still prefers to satisfy the personal ones.

The Us-level makes no personal steps unless it is for the benefit of all, because the individual's interest is of secondary importance to such a person.

The Us-level opens with the programme of family life. In that medium, every member has the opportunity to learn to act primarily in the interest of all members. While living in a family, we are therefore steadily prompted to transcend the importance of many of our personal views and ideas, in order to harmonise with the energy of the group.

If despite all the challenges we remain loyal to our families (except in the case of violence), we will win over our own selves by developing virtues such as self-sacrifice, commitment, responsibility, acceptance and unity-consciousness. Thus living as a single adult provides a rather slow evolutionary pace, because we are deprived of the strongest testing medium – the one bound by family love. Family is therefore a precious evolutionary institution. It is highly valued by the Creator, and He conveyed that attitude through the sacred books.

Leaving our own family due to personal disagreements only, is hardly ever a solution in line with fast evolution. For, changing the environment does not automatically change the aspects of our persona that were unsuccessful in communicating within the family. Sooner or later, even in our new environment, each of our evolutionary deficiencies will surface again, calling for our efforts to polish them.

Regarding the programme of evolution, there is no such a thing as escaping. Postponing, in an endeavour to avoid certain experiences, only makes things more difficult. The same challenges will continue and new circumstances add mass to them, thus more strength will be required to transcend our old weaknesses.

People can easily change the mediums they live in, but positively changing their own selves requires more than that.

SALVATION – BECOMING REAL

Time is accelerating

Earth is not in a cocoon, completely closed to outside cosmic influences and left to evolve as its local planetary medium allows. As an entity in the complex body of a Singular reality, Earth is subjected to the programmes, stimuli and supervision from the higher dimensions. These celestial influences are tailored according to planetary frequency (the level of evolution on Earth).

In the life of a civilisation, when collective curiosity expands beyond their planet and reaches the awareness of possible higher planes of evolvement than the one they have achieved, a significant evolutionary point is marked on the evolvement chart of that civilisation.

These, other, existential planes are other evolutionary dimensions. Each of those dimensions hosts a consciousness level specific to its dimensional energy.

The frequency and the energy intensity of the evolutionary dimensions affect the value of letters, numbers, and the perception of time in their mediums. Hence due to energy differences, there is a possibility that the laws of physics and numerical calculations vary between evolutionary dimensions. Thus our numerical calculations, however scientific and correct within terrestrial standards, might not be directly applicable in some other realities, where the sum $1+1$ might not necessarily be 2.

Time also changes[115], being influenced by the speed of the cosmic currents and by many other factors reaching a given planet. As the speed of those currents increases, time accelerates – and this is what is happening now on our planet. Consequently, there is a pressure on humanity to adjust to unknown intensive energies and so to evolve faster.

Our spiritual strength enhances our physical stamina

To reach the next higher dimension is a matter of the great evolutionary effort of the evolving energy. It is a physically measurable achievement, both energy-wise and consciousness-wise, yet still beyond what the technology of our planet can monitor. However, the evolving energies are supervised by celestial authorities and their mechanisms, and ascension is granted only after a necessary level is attained.

In order for humanity to master interplanetary travel by means of *beaming*[116/146], they need to complete their evolvement through the 7th Evolutionary dimension.

At that level, our bodily cells reach the consciousness coordinates of the brain, and each cell becomes a cell-brain. Such a body is our real, everlasting body. All our evolutionary efforts lead to that stage marked as *perfect (REAL) human*.

It should be noted that for making our body powerful, it is not sufficient to go to the gym. Its real strength grows in parallel to the purity of our essence , therefore parallel to our ability to attract ever higher essence-energy and host it in our cells. Thus, by purifying ourselves and transforming into a better human being, with a plethora of beautiful spiritual attributes, we become even physically stronger.

Nikola Tesla envisaged the point in human evolution when our personal aura, and consequently the magnetic field of a society or of a country, will become impenetrable to any missile. War would therefore lose its meaning since, physically, war weapons will lose their power over us. This world of lasting peace, comfort and happiness will emerge only as a direct consequence of our spiritual evolvement – in which we will unite our brain energies with our bodily energies, and complete the evolution of our essence. Thence, nothing will be able to influence us beyond our *will* since, by then, our *will* will align with the *Total Will*.

Merging matter-energy with spiritual energy

According to the universal classification of energy, our current physical body is composed of energy that is not considered real. In order to inhabit our real body, we need to mature spiritually. Only then can we claim the entire universal energy, which is our essence-energy (spiritual energy or beta energy). That is the energy that belongs to the crude matter of our body, and unless we are saturated with it the body will not become a perfect and everlasting whole. Our current physical body is fragile and incomplete – like an empty shell, with its core (energy) missing.

Evolution is a programme that leads us towards our genuine identity both physically and mentally. The speed of that process corresponds to our ability to receive higher energies than those of the medium we live in, and to accommodate to them. When our potential on the terrestrial plane increases to equal our potential on the spiritual plane, we claim all spiritual energy from the Spiritual totality that belongs to us. Hence our body receives its essence-energy, and can be completed as REAL.

To come to that stage we need firstly to purify ourselves, for which much self-discipline and willpower are required. Then, cells will be able to receive sufficient essence-energy and complete their evolution. Parallel to that, the consciousness of each cell will reach the coordinates of the cerebral consciousness and each cell will become a cell-brain. Subsequent to this immense triumph of our cellular potential, our body will gain its ultimate evolutionary form. At that moment we will rise

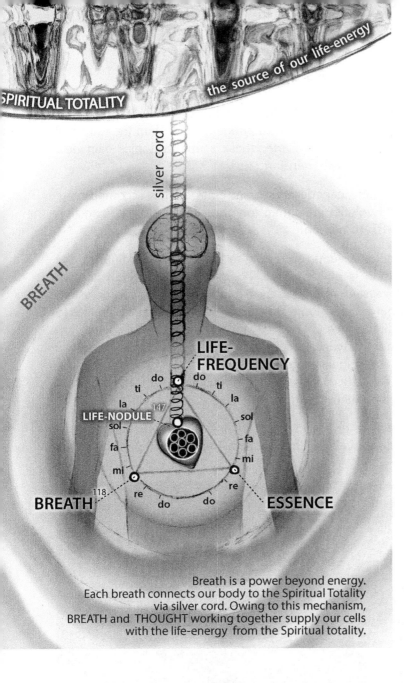

silver cord

BREATH

LIFE-FREQUENCY

LIFE-NODULE

BREATH

ESSENCE

do do
ti ti
la la
sol sol
fa fa
mi mi
re re
do do

147
118

Breath is a power beyond energy.
Each breath connects our body to the Spiritual Totality
via silver cord. Owing to this mechanism,
BREATH and THOUGHT working together supply our cells
with the life-energy from the Spiritual totality.

to the supremacy of the universal proportions, and the might of the universal totality will descend on us.

The universe has been awaiting such a claim from time immemorial. Until it happens, all our cells will remain on *different levels of evolution*[117] – even though they all work together for the benefit of the entire body. This means that if we were now to be subjected to transportation through the process of beaming (up then down), our d i s i n t e g r a t e d physical body would reassemble with some parts missing since our cellular and our cerebral consciousness are still on different coordinates.

Becoming real is our genetic destiny and a true salvation. It comes from absorbing light from the cosmic spiritual source, to gradually reinforce our cellular and cerebral potentials. Thereafter our essential cellular constitution, made of incombustible energy[119], gains the capacity of a vehicle, suitable for cosmic travelling. On those travels, the crude-matter body gets "dismantled" at one planet, only to be reconstructed at another cosmic destination – according to the energy parameters of that new destination. Such a body is necessary for our life in the future, called *Golden Age*, and is programmed into our essence-genes.

Securing the existence in the future

Salvation[120] is one of the concepts introduced in the sacred books, together with the notions of *Resurrection* and the *Last Judgement*[121]. With the universal knowledge that is now available on Earth, these scriptural topics gain new meaning, outside of the Religious dimension.

The *Salvation* of an individual means deserving, and consequently accomplishing, the evolvement of the 7th Evolutionary dimension or the Dimension of Perfection (a perfect human = the REAL human).

In the hierarchy of the solar systems, according to the universal ordinance, the 7th Evolutionary dimension is native to the 4th Solar system. Within its own constitution, the 4th Solar system resembles the evolution of the 14th Solar system (or of the 17th Evolutionary dimension). *This principle of reflection*[122] applies to the main evolutionary dimensions (13th till 19th reflect on 3rd to 9th respectively). In other words, the more advanced solar systems project their evolutions onto the solar systems at the lower evolutionary dimensions, by adjusting the projected energy to the capacity of those lower dimensions – hence preparation and training for the higher dimensions goes on.

The Dimension of Perfection, or the 7th Evolutionary dimension, is the highest evolutionary dimension achievable within our solar system, and pertains to the evolution of Saturn.

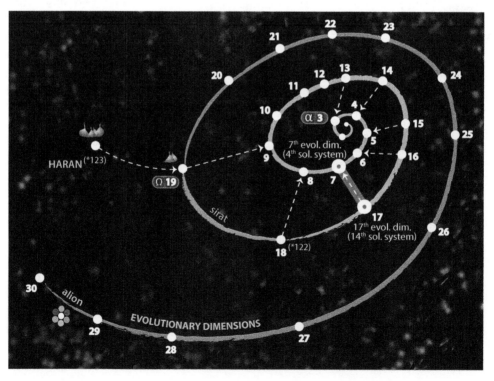

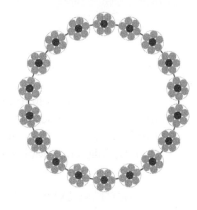

A human being incarnated in our solar system would gradually evolve through the frequencies and energy intensities of this solar medium and, at one point, he/she would exit the programme of dying and reincarnating (4th Evolutionary dimension). Then, in the 5th Evolutionary dimension (*Karena*), preparation for the Dimension of Immortality takes place. After reaching the level of immortality (6th Evolutionary dimension), individuals in our solar system continue to evolve to the level of their evolutionary determined perfection, until they complete the evolution of Saturn. From then on, individuals become sovereign over their own body and their own selves. Only then are they entitled to leave our solar system, and choose their future celestial habitats and tasks on new coordinates within the ordinances of existence.

If an individual does not reach the level of full genetic realisation (7th Evolutionary dimension), does it mean that staying at the current stage of evolution is not sufficient to secure a permanent existence for our evolving energy? If we stick to the authentic meaning of the word *salvation*, and trust the source that has sent us the sacred books and introduced this topic, the answer must be *"yes"*.

Consequently, the *Last Judgement* would represent the selection process on this path, while *Resurrection* would be a necessary shift in consciousness for securing a successful *Salvation*.

Intensifying energy

According to the evolutionary order of our solar system, the lowest level of evolvement is experienced on our planet. For that reason, the lowest ranks of both the Spiritual Plan and the Lordly Order are reflected on Earth. The remaining eight ranks, of each of these two dimensions, are reflected onto other planets of our solar system.

Regarding the type of evolution within our solar system, on the planets before the asteroid zone (Mercury, Venus, Earth and Mars), a so-called *horizontal evolution*[124] takes place through the specific application of religious teachings. Education through the universal knowledge is applied to the five planets after the asteroid zone and that evolutionary path is considered a *vertical evolution*[124]. The final stage of religious training is at Mercury while the final stage of the universal evolution is at Saturn. These two evolvement paths (horizontal and vertical) are symbolised by the shape of a *cross*.

Owing to the current transition to the Golden Age (transition from the Third to the Fourth Lord's Orders of evolution), with some exceptional cosmic influences and assistance given to our planet, the celestial realm has created a medium of an *accelerated evolution*[125] through the energies of the Universal dimension. Hence by enhancing their capacity for receiving cosmic energy, people nowadays have a unique opportunity to obtain all the spiritual energy that belongs to their crude matter body and so to reach the 7th Evolutionary dimension while they live on Earth. If we trust that God never gives us a task we cannot complete, we can then be fully confident in our capacity to achieve this colossal goal.

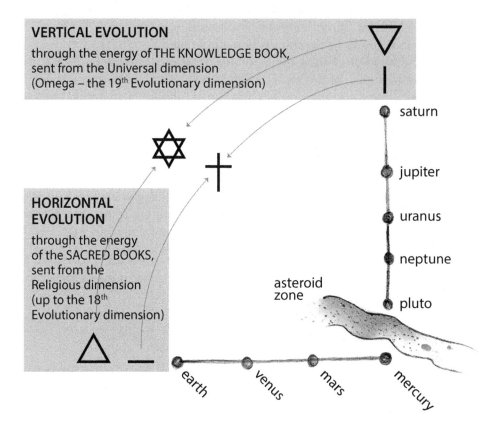

This accelerated evolution assumes an unusually efficient absorption of cosmic energy. For example, the amount of energy that in the past would have amassed on our planet over thousands of years, now needs to be attracted and assimilated much faster. Should human beings significantly underperform on this task, life on Earth would become an increasingly uncomfortable experience – due to the pressure of this cosmic load that we are scheduled to receive now, as an indispensable evolutionary component.

From February 2013, in order to keep up with the increase in the cosmic energy that comes to Earth and not to be suffocated by it, in every instant – in every breath, we would need to receive the amount of energy that in the previous three Lordly Orders would take over 1,000 years to acquire! The celestial realm does its best to empower us to that capacity, and so to enable us to perform an evolutionary leap in every living moment.

Those demanding circumstances are to our advantage. They offer us an opportunity to become perfect humans in this lifetime and so to put the crown on our long lasting evolutionary efforts. Such evolutionary achievement will secure humanity's permanent place in the existential ordinances of the future.

Owing to the immense importance of the current evolutionary stage of humanity on Earth, the celestial authorities are in a state of mobilisation. They are helping us to complete our evolution quickly, and therefore to exit the programme of dying and reincarnating. However, nobody but us can do our homework in this cosmic preparatory school on Earth. Through its intensive curriculum, nobody is selecting us but our own selves; by our thoughts and deeds.

Due to preparation for the Golden Age, there is an imperative for the human population on our planet to attract, assimilate and utilise a humongous amount of cosmic energy in order to evolve according to the celestial schedule for the 20th, 21st and 22nd centuries on Earth. With this fact in mind, we could perhaps spare a second thought for the notions of *Salvation* and *Resurrection* mentioned in the sacred books.

The struggle for survival and therefore *Salvation* has not yet become history on the evolutionary trajectory of humankind – we are not immortal yet! However, never till now have we had a chance to understand the true context of those notions since so far we have solely been focusing on this planet and on the assumption that human beings possess one life only.

With the opening up of the cosmic significance of ourselves, our old paradigms start to disintegrate. Even the sacred texts, present on Earth for 6,000 years, are acquiring a different meaning now. *Salvation* and *Resurrection* seem to be the reality of our time, rather than a random phrase from the holy scripts.

The *Last Judgement* certainly belongs to us – to our logic.

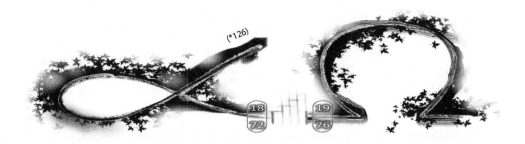

(*126)

It is done. I am the Alpha and the Omega, the Beginning and the End. To the thirsty I will give water without cost from the spring of the water of life.
– Bible; Revelation 21:6

COSMIC INFLUENCES

Visitors to Earth

Beside regular/natural cosmic currents, some specially prepared currents are technologically directed to our planet by the Mechanism of Influences from the 10th Evolutionary dimension, starting with the 20th century. These currents aim at inducing positive changes in our consciousness, and strengthening our cellular constitution in an accelerated manner. With this measure, Earth has started to experience the final cosmic push, in getting its human population ready for evolution through the energy of the Universal dimension. *Personal channels*[127] of intuition and knowledge of people have opened, and energy from various cosmic sources came down to Earth. Even though channelled information contributes in introducing new energy/information to our planet, the channels of people are primarily open to train and test their owners.

The cosmic currents influence us even while we sleep. They endow us with the energy necessary for our development and prepare us for life in the advanced universal dimensions. Thus we are being stimulated by the vibrations of the cosmic curriculum each moment – even a baby is subject to this training. Our cellular vibrational level gradually gets elevated, surpassing the frequency of the terrestrial consciousness. That ascension prepares us for the future.

How about those who, on behalf of the Creator, conduct the programme of life on Earth? Do they ever come here, or only send their influences onto the planet and supervise the impact of those influences from celestial distances? Possibly both, since it is not beyond their reach to choose to manifest themselves as human beings and merge into our society.

Unnoticed, they could also have built a subterranean civilisation on Earth. They might be busy in all segments of the planet, collecting data and finding scientific solutions to the wellbeing of Earth – in order to combat humanity's careless behaviour. Their UFOs might daily circulate in thousands, through Earth's atmosphere and its oceans (USOs) yet remain undetected by terrestrial technology or our eyes. What do we know about reality beyond our perception and, equally so, how correct is that which we perceive if they are invisibly amongst us?

We, human beings, are also visitors on this planet. We have been seeded on Earth by our essence-gene being beamed down (and united with our mother's and father's genes) to make the necessary evolution using a human body. During the process called *dying*[12], the essence-gene, as an energy potential, leaves our body and returns to the cosmic laboratories where it has come from in the first place.

After its frequency is assessed, to determine the achieved level of evolvement, it is then stored and lined up for the next life-experience in the most appropriate body and evolutionary environment.

Cosmic pores are source of the most advanced ideas on Earth

Cosmic currents are manifested on our planet as pores that trigger our transformation through their energy properties. Due to the pressure of these currents, coming from dimensions that are unknown to us, people can be adversely affected by them. Hence, individuals with "insufficient" evolution can become depressed, agitated or even violent. If they do not purify themselves and advance spiritually, in long run, those people might develop chronic illness.

Failing to attract and assimilate incoming cosmic energy, means failing to evolve according to the requirement of actual time. Such individuals will therefore remain prisoners of their personal fears, doubts and conditionings. They might as well leave this planet prematurely because of their inability to harmonise with the energy of time. In this incarnation, they will therefore not complete the evolutionary steps, offered by this cosmic school on Earth.

On the opposite side, there are people who can utilise the energy coming through the open sky. They process it and hence evolve according to the current evolutionary schedule on the planet.

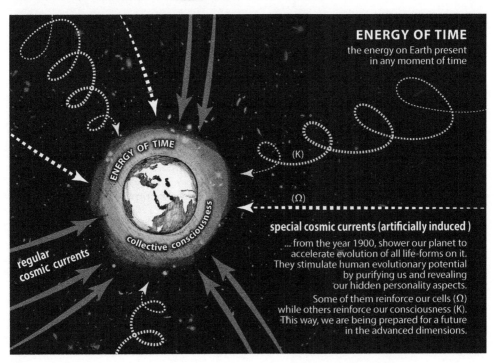

ENERGY OF TIME
the energy on Earth present in any moment of time

ENERGY OF TIME

collective consciousness

(K)

(Ω)

regular cosmic currents

special cosmic currents (artificially induced)
... from the year 1900, shower our planet to accelerate evolution of all life-forms on it. They stimulate human evolutionary potential by purifying us and revealing our hidden personality aspects.
Some of them reinforce our cells (Ω) while others reinforce our consciousness (K). This way, we are being prepared for a future in the advanced dimensions.

Scientists and artists are amongst those who attract the cosmic pores of the highest dimensions through their thought power. As a result of this capacity, the ideas they present to society, by decoding the vibrational qualities of their received cosmic energy, are of uttermost importance to the planet. The energy behind their theories, projects or designs, is a precious gift to the rest of the population, as an exotic energy supplement. The inrush of the special cosmic currents, which started with the year 1900, resulted in an unprecedented eruption of creativity in art, science and technology – hence a great many epochal innovations and art movements took place at the very beginning of the 20th century.

The more spiritually evolved a scientist is, the more revolutionary information, and hence knowledge or technology, can be revealed to them. Technological evolvement on our planet therefore depends greatly on the spiritual level of the scientific community.

Gentlemen, there is an influence which is getting strong and stronger day by day, which shows itself more and more in all departments of human activity, and influence most fruitful and beneficial – the influence of the artist. It was a happy day for the mass of humanity when the artist felt the desire of becoming a physician, an electrician, an engineer or mechanician or – whatnot – a mathematician or a financier; for it was he who wrought all these wonders and grandeur we are witnessing. It was he who abolished that small, pedantic, narrow-grooved school teaching which made of an aspiring student a galley-slave, and he who allowed freedom in the choice of subject of study according to one's pleasure and inclination, and so facilitated development.

The progressive development of man is vitally dependent on invention. It is the most important product of his creative brain. Its ultimate purpose is the complete mastery of mind over the material world, the harnessing of the forces of nature to human needs. This is the difficult task of the inventor who is often misunderstood and unrewarded. But he finds ample compensation in the pleasing exercises of his powers and in the knowledge of being one of that exceptionally privileged class without whom the race would have long ago perished in the bitter struggle against pitiless elements.

Speaking for myself, I have already had more than my full measure of this exquisite enjoyment; so much, that for many years my life was little short of continuous rapture. – Nikola Tesla

ESSENCE-SEED REACHING THE GODLY SELF

Towards the universal power

Living on Earth provides us with an opportunity to evolve, which means to clear our karmas, to purify and elevate our frequency. Interestingly, an individual's terrestrial age is not necessarily equivalent to their evolutionary age. This means that the evolutionary frequency of a child can be higher than the evolutionary frequency of an old person.

Our inner evolvement is facilitated by specific vibrations. The sacred books carry those vibrations from the dimensions of their origin. Sent to Earth by the celestial commands, these books have been playing an enlightening role by purifying and developing us for a long time.

Spiritual development takes place by filling up our physical vessel with spiritual/universal/essence energy. Gradually that energy gives our body its full existential meaning and power. At the same time, we become appreciative of the universal laws and hence we gladly hand over our *individual will*, born of our *partial will*, to the *Will of the Total*.

We advance on our spiritual path by following the light of our essence. However, it is also necessary to construct the thought process triangle of (intellect-logic-awareness), which helps us to utilise the universal vibrations most effectively and to put our lives under supervision. Before we achieve this level, we emanate inharmonious energies. As such, we cannot be sure about our best life-path; we cannot be helpful either to ourselves or to others.

Reaching the essence

In each incarnation we are scheduled to master a new portion of essence-energy; hence the evolution of our essence takes place by our bodily cells being gradually filled up with that energy. When cells assimilate essence-energy in a necessary quantity, the record of that particular dimensional energy/frequency is made in our essence. Thus the evolution of our bodily cells provides the evolution of our essence, which is purely an energy saturation programme entrusted to our 64 billion cells *(cellular awarenesses[129])*.

Before it starts attracting cosmic energy directly, by the power of its awareness, a cell receives cosmic energy via the activity of the brain. (The cellular awareness of the entire bodily constitution grows in this way.) Since received dimensional energy is new to the cells, they go through an adaptation process; which is sometimes painful and can manifest as tiredness or even a health problem. In normal circumstances, these symptoms are temporary.

Cells reflect onto their surroundings a certain amount of the received cosmic energies. This reflection is their universal duty, as well as an evolutionary favour to the individuals who are incapable of directly attracting cosmic energy.

Besides reflecting the attracted energy, a cell leaves some energy for itself in order to achieve saturation, and to register those energy coordinates in the essence. At one stage though, our cells stop reflecting the highest energy that is necessary for the completion of their evolvement.

This occurs when cells become capable of attracting the final energy layers of their energy dimensions directly. Thence, they keep that precious energy entirely for themselves. Due to this phenomenon, nobody makes the energy of those advanced dimensions available to us; nobody reflects it, so we cannot have it served up on a plate. Everybody therefore has to attract the highest energy layers of their energy dimensions directly, solely as a result of their personal capacity and efforts. Even mothers cannot help their children in this task. Nobody can do our evolution for us!

When all cells are filled to the brim with the spiritual energy pertaining to the evolutionary dimension they work through, and when that saturation is recorded in the essence, cells' reflection of any received energy terminates. Essence then undertakes that role, and acts as a more powerful reflection centre than the cells were, since it reflects the evolutionary energy from a higher frequency.

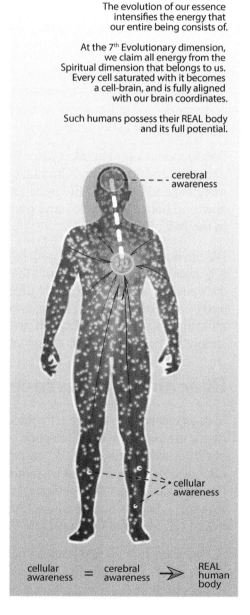

The evolution of our essence intensifies the energy that our entire being consists of.

At the 7th Evolutionary dimension, we claim all energy from the Spiritual dimension that belongs to us. Every cell saturated with it becomes a cell-brain, and is fully aligned with our brain coordinates.

Such humans possess their REAL body and its full potential.

cerebral awareness

cellular awareness

cellular awareness = cerebral awareness ⟹ REAL human body

Owing to the capacity of our REAL body,
we can make cosmic journeys by teleportating ourselves.
During that process, firstly, our physical body dematerialises at one planet.
We travel in the form of our light-body and, as we enter the dimensional
frequency of the destination planet, we instantly manifest a material
physical body. That body is acquired by the unification of our cellular
energy with the energy of the destination planet – and is possible since
each cell of our real body functions as a cell-brain.

Our evolutionary level is recorded in our essence

Each of our cells is an energy station, a fascinating miniature computer. They are biological devices that respond to the universal stimuli. Human being is therefore an energy transmission centre: we receive, process and reflect energy.

When it comes to sharing knowledge, only the information that has been sieved through our logic can appeal to the logic of other people – and hence be transferred. Logic is the bridge. We receive more, and potentially learn more, if we are capable of using logic.

The further we evolve, the stronger the energy we receive and reflect will be. It is therefore not just our kind word or gesture that can benefit others. Our cellular and, later on, our essence-emanations, offer valuable energies as well. Thus by evolving ourselves, we automatically help others around us.

Our essence-personality is reached through the evolution of our essence. It is a process parallel to our ability to attract and absorb spiritual energy by all our cells, upon which a reconciliation of our numerous personality aspects can take place. Polishing inappropriate personality features, developed over our many lifetimes, aims at transmuting those energy qualities and integrating them into a persona that acts exclusively from the value scales of the essence-self. This self is our godly self – bejewelled with the godly consciousness.

Our heart is a life-nodule and the seat of our essence. As such, it is a record-keeper and mirror of our evolution.

THE CHILD OF GOD

Terrestrial toys and the Child of God

Our life programme is encoded in our essence-gene and for each lifetime the essence-gene is sent to a particular evolutionary dimension to take its place in a human foetus. In the unfolding of that programme, once a baby[130] is born, the role of the parents is immense – particularly in childhood.

Parents provide a supportive energy medium necessary for the normal growth of their children. That medium is infused with love and functions on the evolutionary level of the parents. However, gradually and inevitably, children also open to the influences of society.

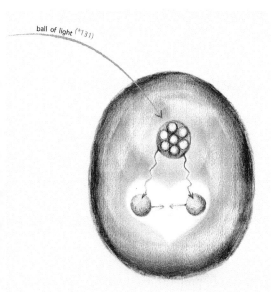

ball of light (*131)

The parental genes have a dominant role till the puberty of a child. Afterwards, the essence-gene of the youngster guides that individual towards experiences necessary for evolution. It is the third element of the cosmic trinity, which binds the mother's and father's genes at the moment of copulation. This celestial element comes as a *ball of light[131]*, having received the agreement, 3-4 months earlier, of its future mother to incarnate as her child.

The energy medium formed in the moments of *sexual climax[132]* is for an instant equivalent to the energy of the universe, so the ball of light can descend most appropriately to the tangible world. This is the godly programme of the natural human's conception on Earth. It is enabled by the automatic application of the existential ordinances. According to those programmes, the essence-genes, kept in the archives of the cosmic life-laboratories, get distributed to the most suitable evolutionary dimensions through the aid of the cosmic Technological dimension.

Has not every sacred book, while declaring how a human being and the world had been created by God, automatically placed the God at the position of a Divine Parent? Was that declaration a mere literary topic of those books or, perhaps, a universal truth – conveyed in the form appropriated to the consciousness level on the planet some millennia ago?

I always test you
to make sure you
positively apply the
information
I let you have

Everything I have created, I introduce to you through frequecies.
I offer you energies to enhance your brain power
and I do so GRADUALLY — otherwise, you could be adversely affected.

The exotic frequency of birds'
songs, and the scent of flowers,
are there to remind you on
the faraway realms
of your future

As God's child on Earth, a human being easily gets distracted with terrestrial toys – like nowadays cars, gadgets or other objects. Hence, human beings simply forget to find out the fundamental truth as to why a life (on Earth) has been granted to them.

The celestial realm is aware of how precious every human being is, since each one of us can reach the power of the universe. Immense celestial efforts are therefore exerted not to waste a single human seed. In order to channel, educate, and most efficiently evolve the energy that operates as a human being, the programme of evolution has been applied.

As a part of that programme, during the last 6000 years, God has been sending necessary frequencies to Earth in the form of the sacred scripts. These divine suggestions from the caring Parent represent His way to prepare us for the more advanced dimensions and the Divine Order. Hence, the guiding and protective energy of the sacred scripts has done more for human evolution than humanity has been prepared to acknowledge up till now.

The missing element in the existential equation

Regarding the existence of God, there is an epic argument between atheists and believers on our planet. With a full respect to the atheists, one observation still remains: they seem unable to make a distinction between the origin and the purpose of the sacred books, on one side – and the application of these books through established religions, on the other. No matter what may be their reasoning, atheists find it inappropriate to acknowledge God's existence and might.

As a matter of fact, both stances are correct from their respective levels of contemplation. This is true for all opinions. They are impeccable, if assessed from the dimensional energy a person operates from. However, the evolutionary task is to approximate all opinions to a common agreement on essential matters.

I myself am an ex atheist. Before I entered university to study architecture, I was much into philosophy – thinking I would become a philosopher by studying it for a degree. By the age of 19, I had read Indian, Egyptian, Chinese and ancient Greek philosophies, and the early works of Carl Marx, as well as the books of Friedrich Nietzsche who proclaimed *Death of GOD* so that godlike man could take the most supreme position. Back then I also enjoyed reading the philosophical writings of Kant, Kierkegaard and numerous existentialists such as Sartre, de Beauvoir, Camus and Gide. Peculiarly, however wide and deep I was delving into the essence of the teachings of those brilliant minds, I missed any serious reference to God.

My excitement over the thought chains of these philosophers and their arguments was of such a proportion that I copied passages from their books into many notebooks, to keep their wisdom closer to me. Nevertheless, all this superb theory was insufficient for me to reach the truth.

Within the countless programmes of the Ultimate Power, some were more successful in reminding me of Its inevitability and dominance. I have therefore managed to recognise a Single Supreme Power and feel comfortable to call it *God*. Likewise, I understood that all events and people I have encountered have been the manifestation of His Divine Order, and that the most logical thing I could do would be to feel grateful for everything I have experienced. Reflected onto my coordinates, the Divine Order has always been pointing the universal truths to me – regardless of my level of awareness.

Now, when I look back, I see how superficial my atheistic view has been, and wonder not why it couldn't serve me any longer. Despite my inclination to search for prime causes, it seemed as if my thought was incapable of succeeding in the given task – due to a lack of spiritual experiences and a one-sided, somewhat academic, perspective on life. However, after a decade-long chain of painful experiences and suffering that came seemingly out of nowhere, my view on life had to enlarge so much that, eventually, while getting rid of my numerous preconditionings, I could notice and embrace God – though not in a religious manner.

In my case, GOD was the missing element in the life-equation that I had been dealing with since my teenage years. Nowadays, I am fully aware of the ONENESS of creation and the sovereignty of the Single Power behind it. That mighty power acts through the hierarchy of the celestial establishments and authorities, while propagating His own Is-ness as the Self of All.

With an expanded perspective on life that included the concept of God (Causeless Cause Behind All Causes), I have rapidly started to clarify my meaning within creation. The reasons behind my experienced events, and the course of the world itself, have also become more understandable.

I am aware that the Existential Programmes, applied on whatever planet, solar system, galaxy and so on – for as long as our evolutionary level allows us to observe – have come from God's workshop and are supervised by His administrative mechanisms. These programmes do not unfold according to the expectations of the life-forms on those worlds and galaxies, but according to the objectives defined in a much bigger picture held in One Mind – One Totality of Consciousness.

We are all one. People are interconnected by invisible forces. – Nikola Tesla

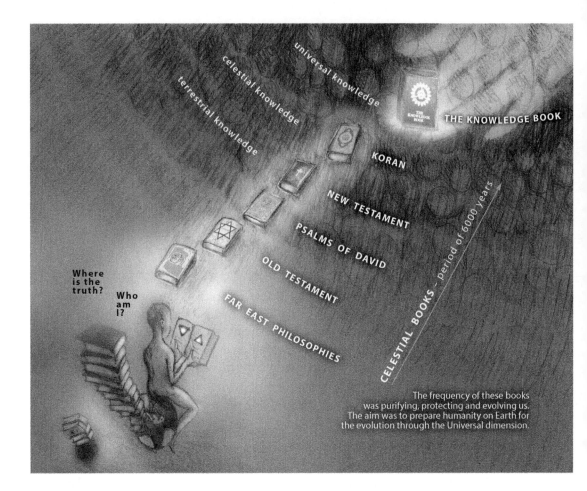

Where is the truth?

Who am I?

terrestrial knowledge

celestial knowledge

universal knowledge

THE KNOWLEDGE BOOK

KORAN

NEW TESTAMENT

PSALMS OF DAVID

OLD TESTAMENT

FAR EAST PHILOSOPHIES

CELESTIAL BOOKS – period of 6000 years

The frequency of these books was purifying, protecting and evolving us. The aim was to prepare humanity on Earth for the evolution through the Universal dimension.

GOD

One is Many

If God is understood as the Power that brings everything into existence – the Power not limited by any law – the Power the substance of which permeates the entire creation – then God is the SINGLE Power that creates, administers and maintains.

Consequently, as God is the one and only existing "thing", everything that we see around us and even our persona is also God. All words in our vocabularies, and our talking, are therefore the utterances of the same source, and as such belong to the one reality of the Ultimate Power. Any possible plane of existence, any governing mechanism, and its name, are equally an expression of this Power.

The *Far East Philosophies* are the celestial books of wisdom on how to live life, revealed to our planet from beyond the Religious dimension. On the topic of creation, they introduced a polytheistic principle, with plurality of deities, each being characterised by some specific high powers and a field of influence. Later on, the new set of celestial books, known as the *sacred books*, presented a concept of the single Supreme God. Even though it may appear that there is a dichotomy between the *Far East Philosophies* and the four sacred books (*Old Testament, New Testament, Psalms of David* and *Koran*) regarding the number of gods, all the celestial books carry the universal truth. In their essence, the *Eastern Philosophies* and the sacred books are complementary rather than contradictory.

The celestial books were prepared in different dimensions, and each of them conveys the energy/information of its own dimension. In other words, contradictory information represents a particular facet of the single truth, declared from specific coordinates. The reality is that deities (gods and goddesses) are supreme missionaries of certain domains – while God, of the monotheistic religions, refers to the Ultimate Power above all deities, prophets, emissaries and any celestial mechanism. Hence, all the celestial books are right in describing the definitive reality and do not contradict that reality.

Altogether, the sacred books listed 999 *Names of God*[133] (*Old Testament* – 300, *Psalms of David* – 300, *New Testament* – 300, and *Koran* – 99) and so indicated certain properties of the major operating mechanisms of the single reigning Power. This would mean that *Almighty, All-Truthful, Lord*, and so on, are the names for the Ultimate Power used at particular dimensions. Each name for God therefore represents a Power dimension.

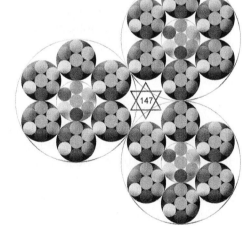

With the energy/information coming from the universal Omega dimension (19th Evolutionary dimension), *The Knowledge Book* clarifies that, including these 999 names, the universal totality recognises 9999 names of God and that only one of them is the direct key to the Ultimate Power – the gate of which will remain closed.

However, the name of God, utilised at the dimension where God is called *Almighty*, consists of *147 words*[134] (147 = 3x7x7).

Every word, of this 147-word long name, stands for one energy channel. These channels possess certain colour range and megawatt power. Their total potential, also fed by 9999 essence-focal points, acts as the source of the essence-energy in the Main Existential Dimension.

The *Second Universe* is another name for the Main Existential Dimension. The same dimension is also called the *Dimension of Life* as well as the *Dimension of Adam and Eve* because Adamkind was created there.

From the Main Existential Dimension, the essence-energy is reflected onto 1800 Mini Existential Dimensions of the realms of space and time within the mega living structure called the *Atomic Whole* – though in a reduced intensity, to suit the evolutions at those dimensions.

HE or IT, or ?

In the universal dimensions and here on Earth, different words are used to address the most Supreme Power. There, in the celestial vastness, the word *god* denotes *a director of a dimension* or *an operational mechanism*. Therefore such a god is not the ultimate one, and could be addressed by the pronoun IT.

The celestial mechanisms are numerous and have their specific operational methods and influence fields. There is a hierarchy amongst them and hence a two-way traffic of energy/information throughout creation takes place (feeding the lower level and providing the feedback to the higher level). The Supreme God therefore makes very informed decisions, and introduces His programmes and orders, or changes them, according to the observed needs.

In the Religious dimension, the pronoun related to the Supreme God is He, because it was the most suitable solution to the level of consciousness of society in the distant past. As a divine suggestion, the pronoun He has served well so far. However, nowadays, because we are exiting the energy medium of the Religious dimension, and transcending the religious consciousness, it is increasingly noticeable that, when it comes to addressing the Ultimate Power, people outside the Religious dimension find it inappropriate to use the pronoun He.

As an omnipresent power, God exists in each of the three modalities at the same time: He, She and It. So, what pronoun to use to address such a phenomenon? A new one? After all that God has done and Is, perhaps, God deserves one such word? To agree on this idea, and on the proposed word, would require an unprecedented congruence amongst people's opinions. Only those of the unity-consciousness might be able to coin such a solely God-related pronoun and to accept it.

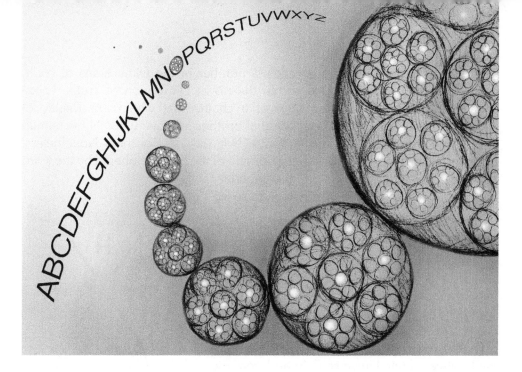

O[135]

The celestial authorities who have been making efforts to evolve us since we came into existence, and who conveyed to our planet all the celestial books, are themselves still endeavouring to get closer to an understanding of the Ultimate Power. They gave to that Power the name *ALLAH*. Some 1400 years ago, that name was introduced to us in the sacred book, *Koran*.

According to *Koran*, it is inappropriate to illustrate Allah in an anthropomorphic appearance. It also means that the properties related to the pronouns He/She are rather irrelevant when it comes to visualising Allah. This divine guidance has shifted the creative focus of the Islamic cultures into the realm of geometric abstraction. Hence, in their artwork, an astonishing depiction of the essential templates and harmonies of creation came into being.

The breath-taking Islamic architecture and craft, reflect to us the order, beauty and endlessness of the Ultimate One. These works of art are an ephemeral vibrational key of sacred proportions pertaining to both the inner and outer worlds.

Even though our elder brothers from the celestial realms are aware that a full grasp of Allah is impossible, their research in that direction is ongoing hence they have reached a scientific understanding of how this Power operates at certain dimensions. They named one of the very advanced dimensions the *Dimension of Allah*[136] and called Allah of that dimension *"O"*. The genetic formula of each soul-seed originates from this dimension, and the ultimate consciousness level of a human seed is up to this boundary (the Dimension of O).

Curiously, there is seemingly an endless number of the Dimensions of Allah, each of them being positioned within their own Dimension of Truth. Those Dimensions of Truth, like the rings of a chain, float within the Totality of Consciousness. According to our celestial brothers, this very Totality is named *Allah* – and is an all-encompassing Neutral Natural Consciousness. Nonetheless, our celestial brothers indicate that the domain of the Power ciphered by the word *Allah* stretches further on, beyond the boundary they have been able to reach and analyse so far.

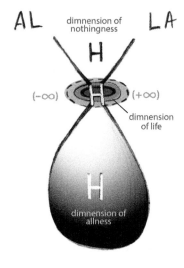

One of the many descriptions of Allah, given in *The Knowledge Book*, depicts that Power at the dimension of a mega cosmic form called the *Atomic Whole*. This Power is a five-fold operational ordinance in which the LA frequency is projected onto two realms – the Dimension of Allness (H) and the Dimension of Nothingness (H). LA frequency comes from the Positive Infinite Universe (LA) and from the Negative Infinite Universe (AL).

The focal point where the Dimensions of Allness and Nothingness meet is the Main Existential dimension (H), or the Dimension of Life. Hence the formation of a vast, yet finite, living structure of the Atomic Whole comes as the result of the order: AL+LA+H+H+H= ALLAH *(AL – LA – H³)*[137].

Evidently, the brains of the friends at the advanced dimensions have accumulated a considerable knowledge about the Power that runs the performance called *Existence*. The great news is that we have matured enough to be updated on their findings.

A solitary experience

No power can ever completely grasp the Ultimate Power – otherwise the Ultimate Power would not be the sole holder of ALL KNOWLEDGE, ALL SECRETS and ALL POWERS.

To be the Highest Power, must therefore be a rather solitary experience – for nobody is on that level, and nobody can ever be there!

Also, as the single owner and manager of all energies/knowledge/consciousness, God cannot offer those aspects in an original intensity – simply because no other power is up to that capacity but Him. This would mean that even the Absolute Power, in the application of Its Might, faces some limitations – if the objective is to maintain everything in existence.

The Sustainer of the entire creation therefore dilutes His own intensity and offers His Might in small doses. Those energies are further reduced as they cascade through innumerable levels. Hence the Ultimate Power ceaselessly feeds and experiences Itself on the infinite planes of Its colossal Is-ness.

Each one of us has a specific relationship to this Power. Even nonbelievers firstly acknowledge God, in order to deny Him. Thus, mentally, there are as many Gods as humans contemplating Him – even though we all relate to the same Omnipresent Creator, the Power above all Powers. The more we believe that we can comprehend God, the closer to Him we feel.

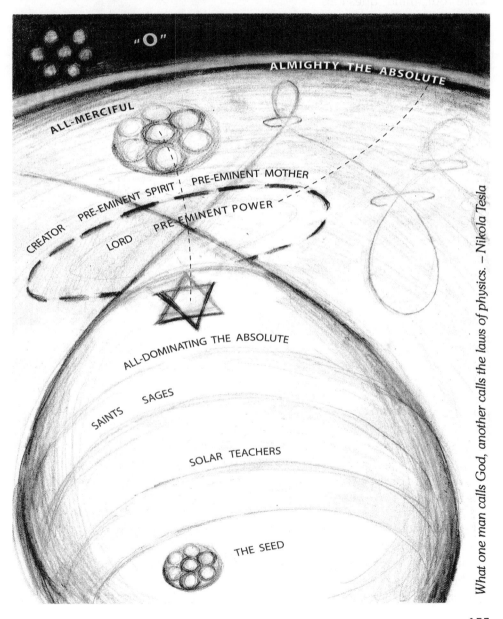

What one man calls God, another calls the laws of physics. – Nikola Tesla

Mind questions – heart knows

God is such a Power whose frequency cannot be packed into the thought boundaries of a human being, though our heart is comfortable in perceiving Him. For, our heart knows and believes, while our mind questions in order to believe and accept. Both stances are equally precious. However, they could hardly be more opposite, hence the evolutionary task to harmonise them is truly humongous.

Whether we like it or not, acknowledge it or not, accept it or not – we live in a Totality created by a Power that has kindly and initially introduced Itself to us by the word *God*; in the sacred books received through divine emissaries known as the Holy Prophets. Throughout the singularity of God's creation, all systems, orders and ordinances are under His ultimate authority; and that is the truth stretching through eternities – from the past to the future one.

In the age of technology, it is quite likely that human beings on Earth can picture God as a cosmic brain that resembles a gigantic universal computer. By the virtue of the cosmic brain's programming capacity, God's Neutral Consciousness is continuously reflected along innumerable domains. There are codes within codes, programmes within programmes, lives within lives – but one essence that holds it all.

A particle of this magnificent essence-power has been planted into the human seed. This seed, designed by the mastery of His offspring known as Adamkind, carries the biggest potential amongst all living forms hence God has never lost the hope that humans will reach their genetic peak one day (*Adamkind* created *humankind*[138]).

In the light of that capacity, the celestial hierarchy has already spent aeons of time cultivating human seeds, endeavouring to transform them into perfect humans. However, even after we have evolved through the 7th Evolutionary dimension, and integrated the necessary spiritual energy with our physical body, our empowerment will continue – in the advanced universal dimensions, of infinite serenity and infinite living, where God's perfect offspring is eagerly awaited.

God is the lone source of all ideas on how to perpetuate and to advance His creation. His elementary mode of Being is CREATING and INTEGRATING.

As God ceaselessly creates Himself anew, He expands the realm of meanings. At the same time, He generates viable existential models and hence propagates that for the continuation of existence, metamorphosis is a *sine qua non*.

Towards the universal homeland

Are human beings, perhaps, afraid of receiving the full power of their own genetic potential? Whatever the answer is, we could expect that such power can only be earned by responsible, disciplined and humble humans whose essence knows their duty and acts out of it. Thus, at the current stage of our evolution, we are primarily trained and tested on those virtues.

To bring them to light, a correct use of intellect and logic is necessary. If God's continuous objective is to provide life to Himself (to everything He has created), then everything that takes place, primarily and ultimately, serves that objective – even the most unpleasant experiences. If we could filter this premise through our logic, we would not need a blind faith to make us accept an Absolute Power that reigns through Its Own Totality – consequently, over "our" life. Is this a concept indeed beyond humankind's intellectual reach, or are some personality impurities stopping them from grasping it?

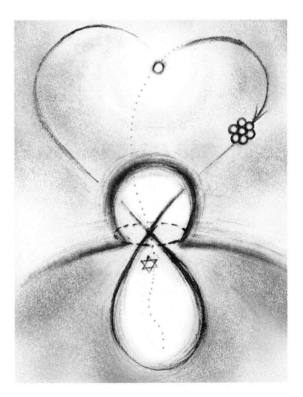

What are the properties we worry about, which we could possibly lose if we offer our insignificance to the service of God's mighty orders? Do we even have a decent enough alternative? Is it, perhaps, to still go after our individual wishes and dreams, and to serve our ego that would gladly rule over our essence till eternity?

For how much longer will ego keep us in its grip, making us remain in the realm of illusion instead of ascending to the realm of truth? Is it really that comfortable to dwell in the realm of illusions? One look at the current condition of our planet regarding the environment, economy, human rights or even the level of our personal fulfilment, perhaps could give us the answer.

God is always ready to empower us, to the limit He knows we deserve at any time. So if we are still powerless, lost or wounded, it can hardly be God's fault. His Existential Programme is a computer programme, which means that particular input generates predetermined output/s. We are the main authors of the input-data related to our lives. The computer's algorithms identify necessary outcomes according to all the relevant data – hence the inevitable circumstances and events which unfold for us. We cannot therefore be cross with life, or God, for what we experience. Instead, we would do better to learn to control the quality of our contribution to the Existential Programme.

If we cannot accept that we are just one character in God's programme, if we cannot consciously serve His Divine Orders, the conclusion is that we have not understood the fundamentals of God's Totality, of life, of who we are. Inevitable therefore, time will be our teacher.

We, the godly seeds, have always been connected to the godly source. That invisible energy bridge will one day take us back to our universal homeland, where our true abode and our true powers are.

Single-God Consciousness

The concept of a divine power dwells in each human being as an aspect of their mental capacity carried through the faculties of the divine awareness, divine consciousness and divine intellect. Moreover, our essence-seed is fed by the energy of the divine source. Without such a genetic set up, and the continuous celestial influences, we would not be able to conceive of the phenomena such as *divine* or *god*, and start relating to them. In other words, God has programmed His seed, and provided a mechanism, to navigate it back to its origin. It is through the programme of our essence-gene, engrafted with the particle of His energy, that we are lead to gradually saturate our cells with that essence-energy, and so become real and godlike.

No wonder human beings have been looking to the sky, and observing forces in nature too, for as long as they have been on Earth. Faced with an uncompromising supremacy of those forces, the humanity has started to worship them and hence to express a committed acceptance of the hierarchy of natural powers. This recognition of the mighty outside-power, has been working as an element of the disciplining and self-training of an individual. Thus by relating to the outer world, and to the unknown, human beings have been developing their own self.

With the arrival of the sacred books on our planet, the notion of God took a dominating role in the shaping of the individual and social psyche – thence a group of people called *believers* emerged.

A believer maintains his understanding and feelings pertaining to GOD through an *a priory* relationship, which only an unconditional BELIEF can provide. Has this attitude, as the faith in GOD upheld for millennia, been cultivated in vain? Or, perhaps, the sacred books on Earth appeared for that very reason – to generate a full acceptance of the Higher Power (Divine Order), as the consciousness of a SINGLE GOD hence preparing human beings for their further evolvement? That further evolvement is through the energy of the Universal dimension, wherein the Ultimate Power is clarified beyond religious contexts.

Would we be able to explain to a child the importance of learning letters? Similarly, would it be appropriate if God fully disclosed all the universal truths, or evolvement programmes that He had prepared for us, while we were at the childhood-stage in our evolution? However, He may well be sad over the fact that at the beginning of the 21st century, humanity on Earth is still struggling at the educational level of the religious frequencies, which postpones the opening of the treasures that await them in the more advanced dimensions.

If parents cannot explain something to a child, life will be a teacher. Under the loving supervision of the parents, the child is therefore left to learn the truth through experiences.

The same programme of learning through experience is also valid for adults. It is applied according to the divine timing specific to each godly seed, and gives them a chance to catch up with their personal evolution, usually in a quite challenging way. Even this method, is a favour to humankind.

Individuals today, endorsed with considerable technological advancement, could also wonder about the cosmic technology that has bestowed the sacred books on our planet. Equally so, we could debate on the miracles performed by the Holy Prophets, by considering those miracles the holographic performances of the higher dimensions.

Evidently, over the millennia, the understanding of the Divine Power has changed and will continue to change. Nevertheless, we swim in the infinity of this Power. The paradox of the Journey is that we are getting both closer and more distant from our target – for such is the trajectory through the nested infinities. Time and space, as we know them, will disappear but our path will not get shorter.

> We are living in an age of unprecedented technical achievement leading to a more and more complete mastery of the forces of nature and annihilation of time and space. – Nikola Tesla

Completing the circle

Talking about GOD, the sacred books have enriched our vocabulary by the words such as *Lord*, *Creator*, *Almighty* and *Allah*, and listed their numerous attributes. Each letter of these holy names is a vibrational key, in resonance with the energy of the dimension of its origin. To reach the frequency of these names is a matter of evolution. For, according to the evolvement chart of a human being, we are to become the Holy Ones and the Lords, and that quality has been introduced to us by the vibrations of the sacred words.

The time is coming when the mystery behind these Names will be revealed. Are we ready to accept their descriptions given from the Universal dimension, which clarifies those Names as the ciphers related to the operational orders of certain cosmic mechanisms and dimensions? If we are, we could perhaps picture those powers as the eternal governing mechanisms of particular cosmic domains. Certainly, thousands of years ago we were not able to postulate such a concept.

A deeper scientific understanding of the genesis and unfolding of creation, in the future could well lead to the identification of particular constants and laws that would call for a rational recognition of those supreme powers and their hierarchy.

Owing to the level of planetary consciousness at the time the sacred books were revealed, they could only hint on some universal truths. Fourteen centuries have passed since the last of them, *Koran*, was given to the planet, and humanity has progressed a lot meanwhile. Are we ready to recognise God and the divine authorities beyond the religious arena, by understanding that their domains are wider than the applied plans of the religious training programme? Are we ready to take ourselves to the universal consciousness?

Are we happy to leave all our fears, negativities and ego behind, and serve the orders of the universe – while accepting the absolute sovereignty of the single power, however we choose to name it and whatever pronoun we associate with it? Are we ready to transcend our own selves and, as better human beings, manifest a better world?

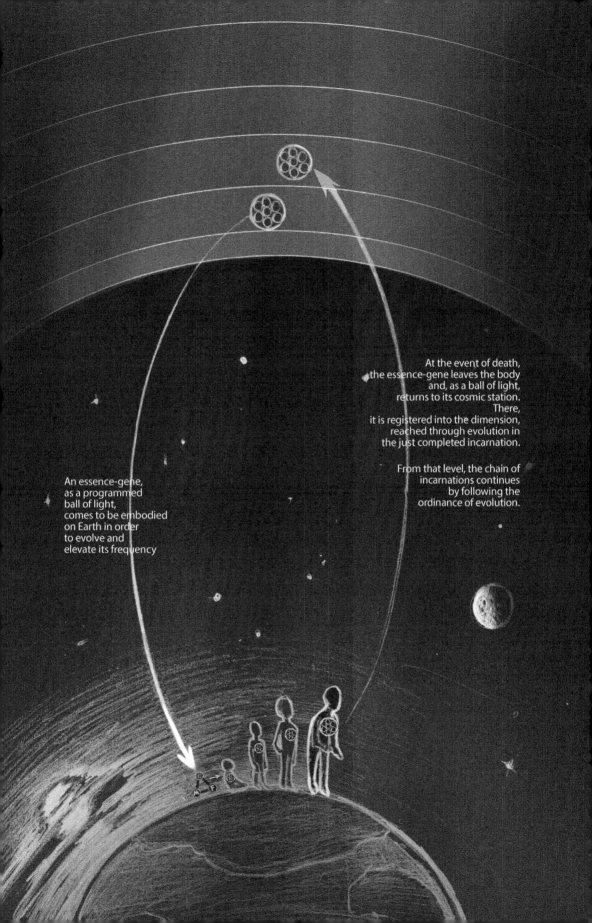

At the event of death,
the essence-gene leaves the body
and, as a ball of light,
returns to its cosmic station.
There,
it is registered into the dimension,
reached through evolution in
the just completed incarnation.

From that level, the chain of
incarnations continues
by following the
ordinance of evolution.

An essence-gene,
as a programmed
ball of light,
comes to be embodied
on Earth in order
to evolve and
elevate its frequency

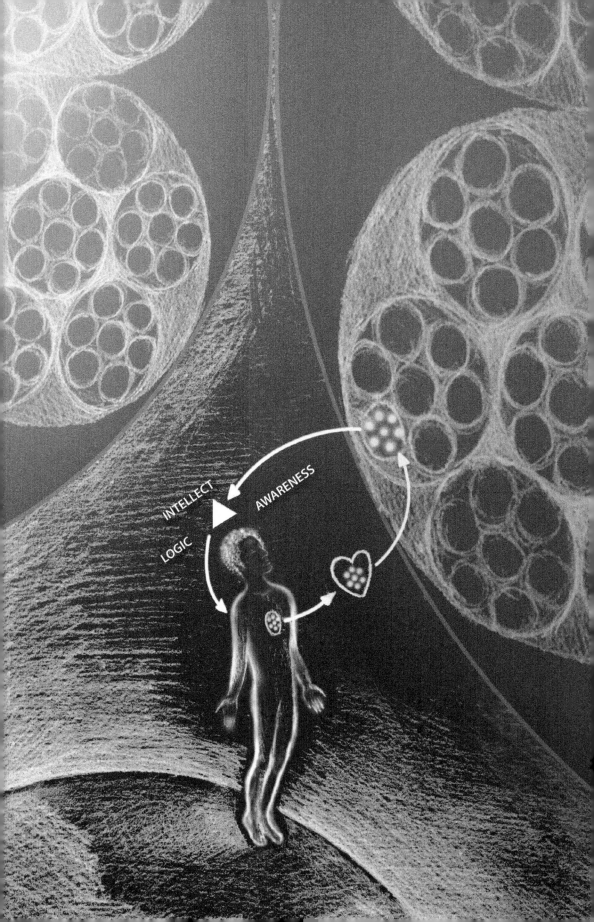

The answers to those
questions can be found
if we ponder upon them
deeply and sincerely enough.

The objective of the Divine Plan
and our individual evolutionary
objective are the same. That one
objective is for us to complete the circle
of our evolvement, by merging the spiritual
and material aspects of our being, and as
such an integrated power to return to the realms
of light. Our essence-gene will by then process all
the necessary frequencies, and manifest the stage of
definitive human perfection. The Golden Age on this
planet will be built by such a human being, and belongs to
such a human being only.

When the godly seed, that we are, on its evolutionary trajectory
consciously reaches its essence-source, two vastnesses, micro and
macro, will fall into one another – forever.

ENDNOTES

A. ENDNOTES RELATED TO "THE KNOWLEDGE BOOK"

The terminologies listed in the Notes are explained in *The Knowledge Book*, and often in numerous chapters. Hence, the suggested messages are not necessarily the only messages in *The Knowledge Book* where one can read about the listed expressions.

1.   OUR REAL DIMENSION is the stage which human beings reach, after the energy of their physical body (concrete energy) merges with the abstract energy of the essence source that belongs to them – Fascicule 23, message: IT IS ANSWER TO THE CHAINS OF THOUGHT, page 346-347.

2.   ESSENCE-GENE is a carrier of the existential cipher and the existential programme of an individual. These genes are connected to the Spiritual consciousness and are not genes known to terrestrial science. – Fascicule 36, message: IT IS ANSWER TO THE CHAINS OF THOUGHT, page 582; Supplement 3, message: IT IS EXPLANATION ABOUT THE ESSENCE EVOLUTION AND THE SPIRIT, page 990-991.

3.   ESSENCE is the power potential that maintains our life by attracting life-energy from the Spiritual Plan. The augmentation of this potential prompts the evolution of our cellular awareness. Essence evolves until it equalises its own potential within the crude matter body, through which it operates, with the potential that belongs to that body and that is within the Spiritual totality, to which it is connected. Through the evolution of Essence, crude matter body is spiritualised and therefore empowered. – Fascicule 24, message: ESSENCE, page 371-372; message: OUR ESSENCE, page 372; Supplement 3, message: IT IS EXPLANATION ABOUT THE ESSENCE EVOLUTION AND THE SPIRIT, page 990-991.

4.   CELESTIAL INFLUENCES – Fascicule 49, message: INFLUENCES AND YOUR PLANET, page 841.

5.   COSMIC CURRENTS are specially prepared influences sent to our planet from the 10th Evolutionary dimension, to render human being conscious and revitalise their physical constitution. These currents help unify spirit and matter. They also accelerate evolution of all life forms on Earth. – Fascicule 26, message: THE COSMIC RESURRECTION, page 388-389.

6.   BRAIN of a human is connected to the Spiritual totality, via an energy line called the *silver cord*. This connection, which progresses with the augmentation of our brain power and the purity of our thoughts, provides life-energy to our cells and leads them to completion of their evolution (according to the evolution of our Essence). – Fascicule 37, message: UNIVERSAL COMMUNICATION AND REVELATION, page 604-605.

7.   IMMORTALITY – is reached at the 6th Evolutionary dimension, for which we are prepared in the 5th Evolutionary dimension, called *Karena* – Fascicule 17, message: STELLAR SOUNDS, page 243-244.

8. **CREATION OF A SINGLE CELL** – Fascicule 23, message: UNIVERSE-ANIMAL-HUMAN, SECTION 2; page 340-345; Fascicule 11, message: IT IS KNOWLEDGE ABOUT EXISTENCE GIVEN FROM THE REALM OF ANGELS, page 145-147; Fascicule 36, message: PRIVATE CONNECTION, page 587-589.

9. **SPIRITUAL TOTALITY** is an energy totality beyond dimensions. The Spiritual Plan reflects these energies according to the evolutionary level of each dimension. We are subject to evolution of a particular dimension, until we claim the entire energy potential of our Essence Power. That potential is present in the Spiritual totality and belongs to the dimension whose evolution we go through. – Fascicule 51, message: GENERAL MESSAGE, page 859-861; Supplement 5, message: EXPLANATION, page 1026-1028.

10. **SPIRIT** is the life-power provided to each crude matter. – Fascicule 5, message: OUR FRIENDS, page 62-64; Fascicule 44, message: IT IS ANSWER TO THE CHAINS OF THOUGHT, page 740.

11. **SPIRITUAL PLAN** reaches our planet from the 8th Evolutionary dimension – Fascicule 35, message: IT IS GENERAL KNOWLEDGE, page 556-557; Fascicule 29, message: THE WORLD EVOLUTION PLAN, page 444-449.

12. **DEATH** – Fascicule 2, message: OUR FRIENDS, page 29; Fascicule 5, message: OUR FRIENDS, page 62-64; Fascicule 36, message: PRIVATE CONNECTION, page 587-589; Fascicule 42, message: IT IS ANSWER TO THE CHAINS OF THOUGHT, page 705; Supplement 5, message: EXPLANATION, page 1026-1028.

13. **ASTRAL JOURNEYS** are made by leaving our crude matter body through the silver cord (without dying) and travelling like we do when we dream while sleeping – Supplement 5, message: EXPLANATION, page 1026-1028.

14. **SILVER CORD** – A spiritual energy line that connects our crude matter body to its spiritual potential in the Spiritual totality. This potential is determined for each evolutionary dimension and made available by the Spiritual Plan. The functioning of the entire cellular constitution of our body is provided by the energy attracted through the silver cord, which is the focal point of the brain. – Fascicule 2, message: OUR FRIENDS, page 29; Fascicule 36, message: PRIVATE CONNECTION, page 587-589; Supplement 5, message: EXPLANATION, page 1026-1028.

15. **12th EVOLUTIONARY DIMENSION** corresponds to the 48th Energy dimension, and belongs to the 11th Solar dimension – Fascicule 22, message: EXPLANATION, page 324-325; Fascicule 44, message: SOLAR SYSTEMS – EVOLUTION – ENERGY AND SOLAR DIMENSIONS, page 731-735.

16. **64 BILLION CELLS** is the approximate amount of cells that bring us into existence – Fascicule 11, message: YOUR SECRET, page 148-149.

17. **PERFECT HUMAN BEING** is the one who has completed the evolution of the 7th Evolutionary dimension – Fascicule 40, message: INTELLECT – ESSENCE HEART – GENUINE HUMAN, page 594; Fascicule 48, message: IT IS MESSAGE FROM THE LORD OF THE REALMS, page 805-807.

18. **SOLAR SYSTEMS** – Fascicule 39 message: SOLAR SYSTEMS AND DIMENSIONS, page 634-635.

19. **GALAXIES, UNIVERSES** – Fascicule 10, message: NOTICE FROM THE SECTION OF THE UNIFICATION OF MATTER BY THE COMMAND OF THE

CENTRAL SYSTEM, page 136-140; Fascicule 30, message: THE CALCULATION OF THE MESSAGE IN ACCORDANCE WITH GALACTIC CALCULATIONS, page 468-470.

20.   CELESTIAL HIERARCHY is a scale of celestial establishments that supervise, govern and perpetuate life forms according to the Divine Plan and Divine Orders – Fascicule 51, message: THE HIERARCHICAL SCALES AND THEIR OPERATIONAL ORDERS, page 862-866.

21.   DIMENSION OF EVOLUTION, or the Dimension of the All-Dominating the Absolute, is one of three natural dimensions of the Crystal Gürz – the other two are the Universe of Light and the Second Universe. The Dimension of Evolution is a dimension of space and time, where orders of evolution take place. – Fascicule 35, message: IT IS GENERAL MESSAGE TO THE CHAINS OF THOUGHT, page 565-566.

22.   SOUL SEED is created of three components: Soul seed, Energy seed and Anti-Matter; and is the result of the Lordly Dimension and the Spiritual Plan collaborating with the Creator in the Second Universe (triple action - trinity) – Fascicule 23, message: MECHANISM OF LORDS AND ITS EMBLEM, page 349-350; Fascicule 35, message: IT IS GENERAL KNOWLEDGE, page 556-557.

23.   LA – AL; LA frequency is the frequency of existence; the resulting vibration of particular sound (and colour) tones. LA frequency coming from the Infinite Positive Universe unites with the LA frequency (AL) coming from the Infinite Negative Universe and forms the Existential dimension – Fascicule 35, message: IT IS GENERAL MESSAGE TO THE CHAINS OF THOUGHT, page 565-566; message: IT IS ANSWER TO THE CHAINS OF THOUGHT, page 567.

24.   SECOND UNIVERSE is the birth-place of crude matter (according to the ancient Programme of Energy Formation), and the birth-place of Adamkind. This dimension, to which the phenomenon of the Big Bang relates, is considered the Main Existential dimension of the Atomic Whole. – Fascicule 35, message: UNIVERSE OF LIGHT – MAIN EXISTENTIAL DIMENSION, page 554-555; message: IT IS GENERAL KNOWLEDGE, page 556-557.

25.   TECHNOLOGICAL DIMENSION projects Lordly and Spiritual Orders, under the supervision of All-Dominating; it administers all the orders. – Fascicule 25, message: IT IS KNOWLEDGE TO THE PUBLIC CONSCIOUSNESS, page 383-385; Fascicule 35, message: IT IS GENERAL KNOWLEDGE, page 556-557; Supplement 4, message: EXPLANATION ABOUT THE TECHNOLOGICAL DIMENSION, page 1009-1010.

26.   ATOMIC WHOLE, or Crystal Gürz, or the Main Universe, is a manifestation of Godly power as intensified energy in the concrete realm. It is a finite mega living structure made of 1800 Mini Existential dimensions. Each Mini Existential dimension consists of 1800 Universes, each Universe of 18 Cosmoses, each Cosmos of 18,000 Realms and each Real of 8748 galaxies. – Fascicule 10, message: NOTICE FROM THE SECTION OF THE UNIFICATION OF MATTER BY THE COMMAND OF THE CENTRAL SYSTEM, page 136-140; Fascicule 23, message: IT IS ANSWER TO THE CHAINS OF THOUGHT, page 346-347; Fascicule 35, message: THE SCHEMATIC CROSS-SECTION OF A CRYSTAL GÜRZ, page 558-559; message: IT IS CLEAR KNOWLEDGE, page 559-560; message: IT IS DETAILED KNOWLEDGE ABOUT THE GÜRZ, page 560-562; Fascicule 53, GÜRZ DIAGRAM, page 909-910; Supplement 4, message: THE REFLECTION OF THE WHOLE ON THE WHOLE AND ITS

OPERATIONAL PLAN, page 1014-1017.

27.   FOETUS, through its own consciousness light, brings us into existence – Supplement 4, message: IT IS ANSWER TO THOUGHTS, page 1013-1014.

28.   THREE EVOLVEMENT PATHS, according to the Universal dimension, pertain to our bodily and spiritual development and to the development of our awareness (thought) – Fascicule 17, message: MESSAGE FOR PUBLIC CONSCIOUSNESS, page 240-241.

29.   NATURAL ENERGY was formed in the ancient Energy Formation processes, beyond Divine dimensions, and it encompasses Spiritual energy. One of the significant moments in the chain of those primordial manifestations was the emergence of crude matter (Second Universe) and of the first and the only ever Natural Atomic Whole (Gürz Crystal) – Fascicule 33, message: NATURAL ENERGY, page 518-512; Fascicule 35, message: THE MAIN CENTRIFUGAL UNIVERSE, page 563-564.

30.   EVOLUTIONARY DIMENSIONS are ordered according to their frequency scales – Fascicule 22, message: EXPLANATION, page 324-325; Fascicule 38, message: IT IS GENERAL KNOWLEDGE, page 619-620.

31.   DIVINE PLAN, from the Dimension of the Almighty, keeps the Lordly energies in a hierarchical order – Fascicule 26, message: EXPLANATION OF REINCARNATION BY THE EVOLUTIONARY ORDINANCE, page 402-404.

32.   NOBLE ESSENCE-GENES – Fascicule 18, message: SPECIAL QUESTION OF THE GROUP, page 261-262; Fascicule 42 message: IT IS CLEAR KNOWLEDGE, page 693.

33.   MECHANISM   OF   CONSCIENCE – Fascicule 40, message: ANNOUNCEMENT, page 655.

34.   DIVINE JUSTICE MECHANISM – Fascicule 42, message: IT IS CLEAR KNOWLEDGE, page 693-694.

35.   REINCARNATION – Fascicule 18, message: THE HUMAN AND GENE TRANSFERS, page 257; Fascicule 26 message: REINCARNATION, page 398-399; message: IT IS EXPLANATION OF REINCARNATION BY THE SUPREME RANK IN CONFORMITY WITH THE PUBLIC CONSCIOUSNESS, page 400-402; message: EXPLANATION OF REINCARNATION BY THE EVOLUTIONARY ORDINANCE, page 402-404.

36.   CELL-BRAIN is the peak result in evolution of each of our bodily cells – which they reach when they get in direct contact with our brain; when the cellular and cerebral awareness/consciousness become equivalent – Fascicule 45, message: IT IS NOTICE FROM THE REALITY OF UNIFIED HUMANITY, page 746-747; Supplement 3, message: IT IS EXPLANATION ABOUT THE ESSENCE EVOLUTION AND THE SPIRIT, page 990-991.

37.   EMITTING THE ESSENCE-ENERGY – Fascicule 42, message IT IS CLEAR KNOWLEDGE, page 693-694.

38.   COSMIC GENETIC ENGINEERING – Fascicule 18 message: WE ARE UNIFYING YOUR WORLD THROUGH GENE TRANSFERS, page 259-260; message: THE METHOD OF ENGRAFTMENT, page 260-261.

39.   6 ESSENCE-GENES OF THE GOLDEN AGE (also called the *SIXES*) – Fascicule 18, message: WE ARE UNIFYING YOUR WORLD THROUGH GENE TRANSFER, page 259-260; message: THE SIXES, page 263-264;   message: THE AGREEMENT MADE WITH THE SIXES, page 265-266; Fascicule 23, message: UNIVERSE-ANIMAL-HUMAN, SECTION 9, page 344; Fascicule 27, message: THE SIXES AND THE UNIFIED FIELDS, page 416-417; Fascicule 36 message: THE ARCHIVE OF THE SIXES HAS BEEN OPENED, EXPLAINED, page 582-584.

40.   WE ARE ALL BROTHERS AND SISTERS – Fascicule 52, message: KNOWLEDGE ABOUT THE ESSENCE-GENES, page 886-887.

41.   (Ω), Omega, stands for the influences coming to our planet from the OMEGA dimension (19th Evolutionary dimension; 76th Energy dimension). These currents are consciousness reinforcement agents. All 9 layers of the Omega dimension were gradually opened to our planet in the period 1986-2000. – Fascicule 43, message: IT IS GENERAL KNOWLEDGE, page 721-723; Fascicule 44, message: IT IS CLEAR KNOWLEDGE, page 730-731; Fascicule 50, message: IT IS CLEAR KNOWLEDGE, page 855-856.

42.   (K) stands for the influences coming to our planet from the KÜRZ (the Dimension of Truth) – these cosmic currents reinforce cellular constitution – Fascicule 43, message: CURRENTS AND THEIR CHARACTERISTICS, page 715-716; Fascicule 46, message: KÜRZ, page 767-769; message: TOTALITIES OF ALL-TRUTHFUL AND DIMENSIONS OF TRUTH, page 772-775.

43.   ASCENSION – Fascicule 22, message: DETAILED EXPLANATION ABOUT ASCENSION, page 327-328; Supplement 2, message: IT IS ANSWER TO THE CHAINS OF THOUGHT, page 986.

44.   INSPIRATION – Supplement 4, message: INFLUENCES AND PROJECTIVE POWER MECHANISM, page 1007-1009.

45.   CELLULAR AWARENESS OF CRUDE MATTER – Fascicule 40, message: AWARENESS AND EVOLUTION OF CRUDE MATTER, page 655-657.

46.   PARALLEL RECORD, to the knowledge archive of our brain that is enriched during our incarnation chains, is kept in the diskettes of the System. All our thoughts are also recorded by the computer system of the cosmic Technological dimension, and answers are sent to our brain signals. – Fascicule 25, message: IT IS KNOWLEDGE FOR THE PUBLIC CONSCIOUSNESS, page 383-385; Fascicule 37, message: UNIVERSAL COMMUNICATION AND REVELATION, page 604-605.

47.   1+1≠2; Each dimension has its own vibrational medium (frequency layers) that determines the value of numerical units they use – Supplement 2, message: IT IS ANSWER TO QUESTIONS, page 980.

48.   ATOMIC BOND (7X7) – Fascicule 14, message: EXPLANATION, page 195; message: THE ATOMIC WHOLE, page 196-197.

49.   SOUND FREQUENCY OF ATOMIC WHOLE – Fascicule 18, message: UNIVERSE AND MUSIC – RETURN, page 267-269.

50.   BIOLOGICAL COMPUTER – Fascicule 10, message: GENERAL MESSAGE, page 132; Fascicule 11, message: COMMAND FROM THE SUPREME ONE, Article 10, page 149.

51. SECRETS OF THE UNIVERSE – Fascicule 48, message: IT IS MESSAGE FROM THE LORD OF THE REALMS, page 805-807.

52. THOUGHT – Fascicule 29, message: THOUGHT, page 441-442; message 1: IT IS ANSWER TO THE CHAINS OF THOUGHT, page 455; message 2: IT IS ANSWER TO THE CHAINS OF THOUGHT, page 455.

53. BIOLOGICAL ENERGIES – Fascicule 32, message: IT IS KNOWLEDGE FOR OUR TERRESTRIAL BROTHERS/SISTERS, page 505.

54. POSITIVE AND NEGATIVE INFINITE UNIVERSES – Fascicule 14, message: THE ALMIGHTY ENERGY FOCAL POINT, page 198-199.

55. CELESTIAL BOOKS, revealed through the direct Channel of the Lord (the Alpha Channel), have been major purification and enlightenment agent over the period of the last 6000 years. They are: *Far East Philosophies, Old Testament, Psalms of David, New Testament* and *Koran*. As one energy totality, they are loaded onto each letter of *The Knowledge Book* together with the energy from the Second Universe. – Fascicule 4, message: OUR FRIENDS, page 43-44; message: NOTICE TO OUR TERRESTRIAL BROTHERS/SISTERS, page 49-50; Fascicule 50, message: IT IS GENERAL MESSAGE, page 855-856; Fascicule 52, message: PRIVATE MESSAGE, page 880-882.

56. SPEED OF THOUGHT VERSUS SPEED OF LIGHT – Fascicule 5, message: NOTICE TO OUR TERRESTRIAL BROTHERS/SISTERS, page 60-62; Fascicule 10, message: IT IS SPECIAL MESSAGE TO CERTAIN CHAINS OF THOUGHT, page 141-142.

57. LIGHT-YEAR – Fascicule 8, message: NOTICE ABOUT THE LIGHT YEAR, page 103-104.

58. ABSOLUTE TIME – Fascicule 34, message: IT IS GENERAL MESSAGE, page 535-536.

59. TIMELESSNESS – Fascicule 40, message: IT IS ANSWER TO CHAINS OF THOUGHT, page 662; Fascicule 52, message: IT IS ANSWER TO THE CHAINS OF THOUGHT, page 889.

60. BETA NOVA is the first planet, and the nucleus-World, of the future Beta Gürz that will gather super humans. – Fascicule 45, message: it is GENERAL KNOWLEDGE, page 758-758; Fascicule 46, message: IT IS EXPLANATION ABOUT BETA NOVA, page 762-763; message: EXPLANATION, page 769; message: IT IS KNOWLEDGE FOR THE INTEGRATED CONSCIOUSNESS, page 769-770; message: IT IS MY ADDRESS TO MY HUMAN WHO HAS BECOME HUMAN, IT IS MY DIRECT UTTERANCE, page 770-771; Fascicule 51, message: ANSWER TO THE PRIVATE QUESTION, page 868-870; message: IT IS ANSWER TO THE CHAINS OF THOUGHT, page 871-872.

61. EGO – Fascicule 12, message: EGO – JEALOUSY, page 163-164.

62. LORDLY ORDERS OF EVOLUTION ON EARTH are 4 periods of approximately 2000 years each. The last one, the 4th Order of the Lord, is called the *Golden Age* and has started to be built from the year 2000AD. – Fascicule 29, message: THE WORLD EVOLUTION PLAN, page 444-449; Fascicule 51, message: GENERAL MESSAGE, page 859-861; Supplement 4, message: EXPLANATION ABOUT THE TECHNOLOGICAL DIMENSION, page 1009.

63.   LOVE IS A POWERFUL VIBRATION – Fascicule 12, message: LOVE, page 174; Fascicule 24, message: TRUE LOVE, page 369-370.

64.   FREQUENCY – Fascicule 21, message: IT IS ANSWER TO THE CHAINS OF THOUGHT, page 317; Fascicule 34, message: IT IS ANSWER TO THE CHAINS OF THOUGHT, page 537.

65.   SUPPLEMENTATION with the frequency of love via cosmic Mechanism of Influences – Fascicule 36, message: IT IS ANSWER TO THE CHAINS OF THOUGHT, page 590.

66.   ENERGY FORMATION PROCESSES – Fascicule 39, message: FORMATION OF ENERGY, page 638-639; message: EVOLUTION OF ENERGY, page 639.

67.   OMEGA DIMENSION – Fascicule 29, message: OMEGA, page 449-450; message: OUR FRIENDS, page 450; Fascicule 38, message: NINETEENTH DIMENSION "OMEGA", page 628-630.

68.   DIVINE ORDER – Fascicule 34, message: DIVINE ORDER, page 542-545.

69.   KARMA – Fascicule 30, message: WHAT IS KARMA, page 459-460.

70.   NEGATIVE THOUGHTS return to the sender – Fascicule 4, message: TO OUR TERRESTRIAL BROTHERS/SISTERS, page 52-53; Fascicule 15, message: SPECIAL NOTICE OF THE CENTER, page 206; Fascicule 40, message: IT IS KNOWLEDGE FOR THE INTEGRATED CONSCIOUSNESSES, page 652.

71.   OBSESSION – Fascicule 14, message: IT IS CLEAR KNOWLEDGE ABOUT OBSESSION, page 203-204; Supplement 4, message: IT IS SPECIAL MESSAGE TO INTEGRATED ESSENCE-HEARTS, page 1011-1012.

72.   EQUILIBRIUM, based on Universal Laws, is maintained through a system of influences – Fascicule 40, message: IT IS KNOWLEDGE FOR PUBLIC CONSCIOUSNESS, page 650-651.

73.   ANXIETY – Fascicule 48, message: PRIVATE MESSAGE, page 809-810.

74.   RESURRECTION – Fascicule 26, message: THE COSMIC RESURRECTION, page 388-389.

75.   HAPPY WORLD of the morrows will be a world of peace and justice, established on the Order of the Golden Age – Fascicule 38, message: IT IS CLEAR KNOWLEDGE, page 622; Fascicule 40, message: IT IS ANSWER TO THE CHAINS OF THOUGHT, page 664; message: IT IS NOTICE TO THE WORLD PLANET, page 653.

76.   RIVER OF INJUSTICE; evolutionary rewards are not earned until we cross this river – Fascicule 38, message: 9/9/1989 IT IS MY ADDRESS TO MY HUMAN WHO HAS BECOME HUMAN, IT IS MY DIRECT UTTERANCE, page 625.

77.   THE SKY IS OPEN so that all terrestrial cells can receive energies of higher dimensions in a faster way; even the ozone hole serves that purpose – Fascicule 49, message: PRIVATE MESSAGE, page 832.

78.   MECHANISM OF INFLUENCES projects the artificially prepared cosmic energy onto our planet; from the 10th Evolutionary dimension, via the Left Dimension of our Sun – Fascicule 9, message: MECHANISM OF INFLUENCES, page 121-123; Fascicule 11, message: GENERAL MESSAGE, page 157; Supplement 4, message: INFLUENCES AND PROJECTIVE POWER MECHANISM, page 1007-1009.

79.   HUMAN EVOLUTION ON EARTH – Supplement 5, message: THE IMMUTABLE FORMULA OF HUMAN EVOLUTION, page 1030-1031.

80.   SOLAR DIMENSIONS – Fascicule 44, message: SOLAR SYSTEMS – EVOLUTION – ENERGY AND SOLAR DIMENSIONS, page 731-735; message: IT IS SUPPLEMENTARY KNOWLEDGE, page 735-736.

81.   7 LAYERS OF TERRESTRIAL KNOWLEDGE – Fascicule 29, message: THE WORLD EVOLUTION PLAN, page 444-449.

82.   7 TERRESTRIAL – 7 CELESTIAL – 7 UNIVERSAL LAYERS OF KNOWLEDGE – Fascicule 22, message: IT IS ANSWER TO THE CHAINS OF THOUGHT, page 323-324; message: LET US EXPLAIN THE KNOWLEDGE WE HAVE GIVEN IN MORE DETAIL, page 325-326.

83.   KARENA is the 5th Evolutionary dimension – Fascicule 16, message: KARENA, page 225; message: MESSAGE GIVEN BY THE PRE-EMINENT SPIRIT, page 226-227; Fascicule 17, message: STELLAR SOUNDS, page 243-244; Fascicule 22, message: IT IS ANSWER TO THE CHAINS OF THOUGHT, page 323-324.

84.   ASTEROID ZONE – Fascicule 29, message: THE WORLD EVOLUTION PLAN, page 444-449.

85.   NIRVANA is the 6th Evolutionary dimension, or the Dimension of Immortality – Fascicule 39, message: IT IS KNOWLEDGE FOR THE INTEGRATED CONSCIOUSNESSES, page 636-637.

86.   THE KNOWLEDGE BOOK – was dictated through the single universal channel opened to our planet (the Alpha Channel), in the period 1881-1993, to Vedia Bülent Önsü Çorak, in Turkey. Mrs Çorak (born in 1923), also known as Mevlana, is a Spokesperson of the System and is one of the 6 Noble Genes of the Golden Age that have been used for centuries in Cosmic laboratories to fortify the human genome. The identity of Mrs Çorak is revealed in Fascicule 24, message: (NOW I CAN TALK), page 366-367; Fascicule 42, message: (IT IS NOTICE IN ACCORDANCE WITH THE GENERAL DECISION), page 699-701 and Fascicule 48, message: IT IS CLEAR KNOWLEDGE, page 821.

The Knowledge Book is the Constitution of the Universe, registered in the universal legislations under the number 115-685 – Fascicule 20, message: EXPLANATION ABOUT THE MISSION AND THE FREQUENCY OF THE KNOWLEDGE BOOK, page 294-295; message: IT IS ANSWER TO THE CHAINS OF THOUGHT, page 299-300; Fascicule 47, message: IT IS KNOWLEDGE FOR AWAKENING CONSCIOUSNESSES, page 782-784; Supplement 7, message: IT IS DIRECT NOTICE FROM THE UNIVERSAL TOTALITY CORTEGE, page 1059-1062.

87.   LIGHT – PHOTON – CYCLONE TECHNIQUE employed in *The Knowledge Book*, attracts cosmic energy onto letter frequencies, and so with the energy of each new moment upgrades the meaning of its text; it also adjusts the entire energy intensity of the Book, to the capacity of each reader. Hence *The Knowledge Book* behaves as if alive, and serves as a personal guru (mediator). – Fascicule 36, message: THE KNOWLEDGE BOOK, THAT IS, THE BOOK OF COSMIC LIGHT AND ITS CHARACTERISTICS, page

577-579; Fascicule 40, message: THE LIGHT – PHOTON – CYCLONE TECHNIQUE, page 662-663; Fascicule 39, message THE FIFTH POWER, page 639-640.

88.   **SYSTEM** is a supervising mechanism of the entire Gürz, and a projecting focal point that is in effect from the Dimension of the All-Merciful (Light Universe) – Fascicule 35, message: IT IS GENERAL ANSWER TO THE CHAINS OF THOUGHT, page 571-572; Fascicule 50, message: IT IS KNOWLEDGE FOR THE INTEGRATED CONSCIOUSNESSES, page 845-846; message: IT IS CLEAR KNOWLEDGE, page 850-851.

89.   **GOLDEN AGE** is the 4th, and the final, Order of the Lord; and it will manifest a universal unification. During the transition from the 3rd to the 4th Order, the application of the Salvation Plan during the 20th, 21st and 22nd centuries takes place. These three centuries are called the *Cosmic Age* and are marked by an accelerated evolution, resurrection of consciousness, cosmic selection processes and an ushering of the universal operational ordinances into our planet. – Fascicule 48, message: EXPLANATION ABOUT THE GOLDEN AGE, page 810-812.

90.   **INTELLECT – LOGIC – AWARENESS** triangle is necessary for a person, in order for them to be certain of what to do – Fascicule 40, message: INTELLECT – ESSENCE-HEART – GENUINE HUMAN, page 651-652; Fascicule 49, message: IT IS KNOWLEDGE FOR THE INTEGRATED CONSCIOUSNESSES, page 833-834.

91.   **EXISTENTIAL ORDINANCES** – Fascicule 38, message: IT IS EXPLANATION ABOUT THE ALMIGHTY THE ABSOLUTE AND THE TOTALITY, page 626-628.

92.   **GENETIC PROGRAMME** – Fascicule 45, message: IT IS NOTICE FROM THE REALITY OF UNIFIED HUMANITY, page 746-747.

93.   **WILL OF THE TOTAL** – Fascicule 30, message: IT IS KNOWLEDGE FOR THE PUBLIC CONSCIOUSNESS, page 460-462; message: TRANSMISSION OF THE PARTIAL AND THE TOTAL WILL FROM THE ARCHIVE, page 462-463.

94.   **UNITY – ORDER – HARMONY** – Fascicule 20, message: WE ARE GETTING THE BOTTOM CLOSER TO THE TOP, page 287-288.

95.   **COSMIC TECHNOLOGY** – Fascicule 46, message: TECHNOLOGY, page 763-764.

96.   **COLOURS** – Fascicule 24, message: KNOWLEDGE ABOUT COLOURS AND THEIR FREQUENCIES, page 356-357; Fascicule 34, message: COLOURS AND IN-BETWEEN DIMENSION, page 548-550; Fascicule 54, message: IT IS CLEAR KNOWLEDGE, page 925-926; message: PRIVATE MESSAGE, page 926-928.

97.   **TOTALITY OF CONSCIOUSNESS (ALLAH)** – Fascicule 46, message: DIMENSION OF NOTHINGNESS – TOTALITY OF CONSCIOUSNESS, page 776; Fascicule 51, message: IT IS ANSWER TO THE CHAINS OF THOUGHT, page 870-871; Supplement 6, message: IT IS CLEAR KNOWLEDGE, page 1042-1043.

98.   **HEALING** – Fascicule 20, message: IT IS CLEAR MESSAGE ABOUT HEALING, page 290-291.

99.   **49 SOUND TONALITIES (7x7)** equal one universal musical note – Fascicule 22, message: IT IS ANSWER TO THE CHAINS OF THOUGHT, IT IS EXPLANATIVE KNOWLEDGE ABOUT, THE FORMERLY DICTATED, MUSIC AND UNIVERSE, page 330-331.

100. **COLOUR BLACK** – Fascicule 16, message: ALPHA – BETA, page 231-233; Fascicule 22, message: LET US EXPLAIN THE KNOWLEDGE WE HAVE GIVEN IN MORE DETAIL, page 325-326.

101. **7x7 EVOLUTIONARY TRAJECTORY** – Fascicule 39, message: IT IS ANSWER TO THE CHAINS OF THOUGHT, page 646.

102. **EVOLVING ENERGY** – Fascicule 39, message: EVOLUTION OF ENERGY, page 639; message: THE FIFTH POWER, page 639-640.

103. **SIX-POINTED STAR** – Fascicule 24, message: EACH FIGURE IS A SYMBOL, page 358-359; Fascicule 37, message: DAVID'S STAR, page 613; Fascicule 52, message: IT IS GENERAL MESSAGE, page 876-878.

104. **BEST BY DATE** is applicable for each sacred book – in the sense of the specific time in human history that the Divine Plan anticipated as optimum for assimilating the frequencies of those books – Fascicule 17, message: THE GOLDEN AGE AND THE KNOWLEDGE BOOK, page 237-238.

105. **WORSHIP** – Fascicule 26, message: WARSHIP, page 395-396.

106. **PRAYERS** – Fascicule 14, message: IT IS KNOWLEDGE ABOUT PRAYERS, page 200-201.

107. **UNIVERSAL MISSION** is cyphered into our genes and is activated within a specific frequency of the time energy, different to each person – Fascicule 40, message: IT IS KNOWLEDGE FOR THE INTEGRATED CONSCIUSNESSES, page 659-661; Fascicule 43, message: IT IS CLEAR KNOWLEDGE, page 716-717.

108. **TESTS** of the Terrestrial dimension are structured through six stages – Supplement 7, message: IT IS KNOWLEDGE FOR THE INTEGRATED CONSCIOUSNESSES, page 1053-1055.

109. **MACRO CONSCIOUSNESS** – Supplement 6, message: IT IS CLEAR KNOWLEDGE, page 1044-1045; message: IT IS KNOWLEDGE FROM THE REALITY ARCHIVES, page 1047-1048.

110. **PRISMATIC PATHWAYS** – Fascicule 37, message: UNIVERSAL COMMUNICATION AND REVELATION, page 604-605; Fascicule 42, message: THE UNIVERSAL PRISM AND THE UNIFIED FIELDS, page 705-707; Fascicule 52, message: PRIVATE MESSAGE, page 888.

111. **FIRMAMENT**, a sky-dome over the Earth, is also an uttermost boundary that the consciousness of an individual can reach at a particular moment – Supplement 2, message: FIRMAMENT, page 988.

112. **UNIVERSAL LAWS** determine all processes within the universal totality – nothing occurs on its own but is the result of these laws – Fascicule 48, message: CHAIN OF LAWS, page 803.

113. **SUPREME REALMS** supervise our frequencies – Fascicule 41, message: IT IS GENERAL MESSAGE, page 674.

114. **TWO EVOLVEMENT PATHS** – Fascicule 48, message: CHAIN OF LAWS, page 803.

115. **TIME PROCESSES** and the value of TIME MEASUREMENT UNITS are influenced by many cosmic elements, such as different solar systems, stellar periods, solar winds and cosmic currents that reach certain planet – Fascicule 18, message: EXPLANATION ABOUT THE KNOWLEDGE BOOK AND THE CONTRADICTIONS, page 253-254; message: CLEAR MESSAGE ABOUT THE KNOWLEDGE BOOK AND CONTRADICTIONS, Article 40-46, page 255-257.

116. **BEAMING** – Fascicule 50, message: IT IS CLEAR KNOWLEDGE, page 857-858

117. **DIFFERENT LEVELS OF EVOLUTION** are present among our cells – Fascicule 23, message: IT IS KNOWLEDGE ABOUT THE LORDS, page 351.

118. **NODULE OF BREATH** – Fascicule 36, message: PRIVATE CONNECTION, page 587-589.

119. **INCOMBUSTIBLE ENERGY** is engrafted into our cells and our light body, in the two initial stages of the 5th Evolutionary dimension (*Karena*). However, now, due to an accelerated evolution, 5th Dimensional energy is directly available on Earth. – Fascicule 29, message: THE WORLD EVOLUTION PLAN, page 444-449; Fascicule 51, message: IT IS ANSWER TO THE CHAINS OF THOUGHT, page 872.

120. **SALVATION** – Fascicule 47, message: EXPLANATION, page 784-785; Salvation Plan is a celestial programme of accelerated evolution, preparation and selection, applied on Earth to provide that a maximum number of humans reach the Golden Age – Fascicule 36, message: IT IS GENERAL NOTICE TO THE WORLD PLANET, page 579; Supplement 3, message: THE SALVATION PLAN, page 992-993.

121. **LAST JUDGEMENT** – Fascicule 21, message: EXPLANATION ABOUT THE LAST JUDGEMENT, page 307.

122. **REFLECTION OF EVOLUTIONARY DIMENSIONS** – a more advanced Solar System reflects its evolution (evolutionary and energy dimensions) onto a lower dimension, and does so parallel to the capacity of the lower dimension – Fascicule 44, message: SOLAR SYSTEMS – EVOLUTION – ENERGY AND SOLAR DIMENSIONS, page 731-735; message: IT IS SUPPLEMENTARY KNOWLEDGE, page 735-736.

123. **HARAN**, the Power of Fire of the Dimension of Truth (Kürz), is reflected via the Fire planet (Omega) – Fascicule 47, message: EXPLANATION, page 791; message: IT IS ANSWER TO THE QUESTION ASKED, page 792-793.

124. **HORIZONTAL AND VERTICAL EVOLUTION** – Fascicule 34, message: HORIZONTAL AND VERTICAL EVOLUTION, page 541, message: SPIRAL VIBRATIONS, page 547-548.

125. **ACCELERATED EVOLUTION** due to Earth's entering the cosmic reflection field of the Big Bang – Fascicule 43, message: SHOCK WAVES, page 711; message: IT IS ANSWER TO THE CHAINS OF THOUGHT page 712-713; Supplement 2, message: IT IS KNOWLEDGE FOR THE INTEGRATED CONSCIOUSESSES, page 981.

126. **"I AM ALPHA AND OMEGA"** – Fascicule 36, message: IT IS KNOWLEDGE FOR THE INTEGRATED CONSCIOUSNESSES, page 590-592; Fascicule 39, message: SOLAR SYSTEMS AND DIMENSIONS, page 634-635.

127. **PERSONAL OPEN CHANNELS** – Fascicule 36, message: GENERAL NOTE, page 577; Fascicule 37, message: IT IS ANSWER TO THE CHAINS OF THOUGHT, page 613-614; Fascicule 41, message: IT IS GENERAL NOTICE, page 668-669; Fascicule 49, message: GENERAL MESSAGE, page 838; Fascicule 50, message: IT IS NOTICE FROM THE SUPREME MECHANISM, page 847-848.

128. **ATLANTA**, or the Golden Dimension of perfect orders, of highly advanced systems that initiated energy formation processes, Big Bang and Existential Programme. One Atlanta Being has the brain power of 7 billion terrestrial humans. – Fascicule 51, message: IT IS ANSWER TO THE CHAINS OF THOUGHT, page 870-871; Supplement 6, message: IT IS KNOWLEDGE FOR THE INTEGRATED CONSCIOUSNESSES, page 1035-1040; message: IT IS CLEAR KNOWLEDGE, page 1042-1043.

129. **CELLULAR AWARENESS** – Fascicule 11, message: YOUR SECRET, page 148-149.

130. **BABY** – Fascicule 5, message: NOTICE TO OUR TERRESTRIAL BROTHERS/SISTERS, page 70-71.

131. **BALL OF LIGHT** – Fascicule 40, message: IT IS KNOWLEDGE FOR THE PUBLIC CONSCIOUSNESS, page 650-651.

132. **SEXUAL CLIMAX** – Fascicule 53, message: PRIVATE MESSAGE, page 894-896.

133. **NAMES OF GOD** – Fascicule 2, message: NOTICE TO OUR FRIENDS, page 20-21.

134. **147** Words constitute the single real Name of God that will always remain unknown – Fascicule 2, message: NOTICE TO OUR FRIENDS, page 20-21; Fascicule 16, message: ALPHA – BETA, page 231-233.

135. **O**, also known as *Matu*, is a supervising Power of the Dimension of Allah; an Order and a System – Fascicule 23, message: MECHANISM OF LORDS AND ITS EMBLEM, page 349-350; Fascicule 42, message: REPRESENTATIVE DIAGRAM, page 692; message: MESSAGE FROM THE ARCHIVE OF THE PRE-EMINENT POWER, page 708; Fascicule 45, message: IT IS GENERAL KNOWLEDGE, page 758-759.

136. **DIMENSION OF ALLAH** is within the Dimension of Truth (Kürz); its supervisor is Allah (O) – Fascicule 38, message: IT IS EXPLANATION ABOUT THE ALMIGHTY THE ABSOLUTE AND THE TOTALITY, page 626-628; Fascicule 46, message: A KÜRZ TOTALITY, page 773-775; Supplement 6, message: IT IS CLEAR KNOWLEDGE, page 1042-1043.

137. **(AL – LA – H3)** is a cipher of the fivefold operational ordinance (ALLAH) related to the vibration of the LA frequency from the Infinite Positive Universe and the LA frequency from the Infinite Negative Universe (AL) that are projected on two realms: Allness and Nothingness. The triple letter "H" in this formula stands for "Hayat" the Dimension of Life, which emerges where those two vibrations cross; and for the Dimension of Allness (H) and the Dimension of Nothingness (H). – Fascicule 7, message: NOTICE FROM THE CENTER ABOVE THE CENTER, page 92-93; Fascicule 35, message: IT IS GENERAL MESSAGE TO THE CHAINS OF THOUGHT, page 565-566; Fascicule 38, message: IT IS CLEAR KNOWLEDGE, page 620-622.

138. **ADAMKIND CREATED HUMANKIND** – Fascicule 36, message: PRIVATE CONNECTION, page 408-409.

B. ENDNOTES RELATED TO THE BOOK "LIGHT"

139.   EVOLUTION OF OUR CELLS is connected to the evolution of our Essence – Message: THE HUMAN BEING AND HIS/HER CELLULAR EVOLUTION, page 131-134.

140.   HUMAN BRAIN is a mechanism prepared of prototype cellular structure in which cells do not reproduce and do not change – Message: FORMATION OF THE BRAIN, page 136-137.

141.   MIND OF THE HUMAN is a power potential that activates parts of our brain and so connects consciousness and realisation layers. Thought plays crucial part in both becoming aware and becoming conscious – Message: THE MIND, page 137-138.

142.   25% – 75% – Message: THOUGHT AND THE REFLECTIONS, page 97-100.

143.   PLANTS AND ANIMALS ARE POSITIVE – Message: VICIOUS CIRCLE AND COSMIC RESURRECTION, page 128-130.

144.   ACCELERATED EVOLUTION due to the vibrational replicas of Big Bang, which our planet met in a perceivable way in 1962 (Photon Ring) – Message: THE WORLD, COSMIC ENERGIES AND RESURRECTION, page 15-19.

145.   UFOs – Message: UFO, page 142-143.

146.   BEAMING – Message: EXPLANATION, page 143-144.

147.   LIFE NODULE is a unification of Essence (Heart Bond) with Breath and Life Frequency – Message: INFORMATION ABOUT ESSENCE-GENES, page 154-156.

BIBLIOGRAPHY

THE KNOWLEDGE BOOK – ISBN 975-95053-1-2; Third edition 2013, messages received and transformed into writing by Vedia Bülent (Önsü) Çorak

LIGHT – ISBN 978-975-01975-1-2; First Edition, 2007; By Vedia Bülent (Önsü) Çorak

FROM SPACE TO THE WORLD – ISBN 978-605-84813-1-2, First Edition, 2015; By Vedia Bülent (Önsü) Çorak

Lightning Source UK Ltd.
Milton Keynes UK
UKOW05f1502260915

259289UK00001B/3/P

9 781909 323773